A Disciple's Heart

Companion Reader

A
Disciple's
Heart

Growing in Love and Grace

Companion Reader

James A. Harnish

Abingdon Press
Nashville

A DISCIPLE'S HEART: COMPANION READER

This book is printed on elemental, chlorine-free paper.
ISBN 978-1-63088-257-0

2015 2016 2017 2018 2019 2020 2021 2022 2023 2024—10 9 8 7 6 5 4 3 2 1

MANUFACTURED IN THE UNITED STATES OF AMERICA

CONTENTS

Introduction: A Matter of the Heart. 7

1. Where Do We Go from Here?. 13

2. Walking the Way of Salvation 23

3. By the Power of the Spirit 33

4. The Company of the Committed .41

5. On Fire with Holy Love 51

6. All the Way to Heaven 61

Notes. 71

INTRODUCTION
A MATTER OF THE HEART

How is your heart?

After his first visit to our congregation, a local cardiologist sent me a message saying that when people ask his occupation, he replies, "I fix broken hearts."

In addition to his concern for the medical condition of his patients' hearts, he expressed his concern for "hearts that get stepped on, hurt, or otherwise abused." While grateful for the ability to address their medical needs, he lamented his inadequacy to heal the other kinds of pain in their broken hearts.

Providentially, the title of the sermon that Sunday was "Matters of the Heart" based on Ezekiel 36:26: "I will give you a new heart and put a new spirit in you. I will remove your stony heart from your body and replace it with a living one."

My new friend immediately understood Ezekiel's metaphor of the "stony heart." The medical diagnosis is *cardiomyopathy*, a condition I experienced more than two decades ago. The myocardium or heart muscle becomes rigid and is incapable of pumping blood throughout the body. The surgical cure is a heart transplant, something Ezekiel never could have imagined but metaphorically described. In my case, the combination of medical steroids and faithful prayer corrected the problem, but in every case, it is a critical condition that can result in death.

Jesus was diagnosing spiritual *cardiomyopathy* when he quoted the prophet Isaiah:

> *"For this people's heart has grown dull,*
> *and their ears are hard of hearing,*
> *and they have shut their eyes;*

7

> *so that they might not look with their eyes,*
> *and listen with their ears,*
> *and understand with their heart and turn—*
> *and I would heal them." (Matthew 13:15 NRSV)*

No doubt Jesus was familiar with the proverb that says, "Keep your heart with all vigilance, for from it flow the springs of life" (Proverbs 4:23 NRSV).

The Bible isn't the only place to find the metaphor of the hard or stony heart. In Shakespeare's most painful tragedy, King Lear asks the pain-soaked question, "Is there any cause in nature that makes these hard hearts?"[1] Jazz singer Ella Fitzgerald could bring down the house when she sang about "Hard Hearted Hannah" who had "a heart just like a stone / Even nice men leave her alone."[2] There is more than enough evidence in literature, culture, and everyday experience to confirm that to one degree or another, we all face the risk of spiritual *cardiomyopathy*. Sooner or later, we all need someone who can fix broken hearts.

On the Sunday the cardiologist visited us, the sermon drew the contrast between the Reformed tradition, in which John Calvin focused on the brain by putting the emphasis on right belief, and the Anglican-Methodist tradition, in which John Wesley put the primary emphasis on the heart as the center of right relationships. Wesley defined true religion as "a heart right toward God and man."[3] That's why Methodist historian Richard Heitzenrater declared, "The center of this religion is in the heart."[4]

As disciples in the Wesleyan tradition, we have been at our best when we have been in the business of helping people experience the presence of the One who can heal broken hearts. When we have lived in ways that are consistent with our spiritual heritage, we have shared a bold confidence in the power of God's grace to give us a new heart, redirect human behavior, create a community of love and forgiveness, and through that community transform the world. We have proclaimed that the Spirit of God can be at work in our hearts to enable us to love God with all our

> "This is the religion we long to see established in the world, a religion of love and joy and peace, having its seat in the heart, in the inmost soul, but ever showing itself by its fruits, continually springing forth…in every kind of beneficence, in spreading virtue and happiness all around it."[5]
> —John Wesley

heart, soul, mind, and strength and to love others the way we have been loved by God.

The central conviction of this resource is that for disciples in the Wesleyan tradition, the heart of the matter is always a matter of the heart. Building on the work we began in our study *A Disciple's Path*, this resource is a "next step" to encourage disciples to continue to grow in a life that is centering in loving God and loving others. John Wesley called this ongoing growth "Christian perfection" or "going on to perfection." Often it is referred to as sanctification. Together we will explore this process of ongoing growth and the way that disciples with transformed hearts participate in God's transformation of the world.

Jesus commanded us to make disciples. Wherever local congregations are energetically engaged in that mission, lives are being transformed, Christian community is being formed, and people are discovering how they can participate in God's saving work in their community and the world. But this doesn't just happen. Wesley expressed a concern that still resonates today:

> I am not afraid that the people called Methodists should
> ever cease to exist either in Europe or America. But I am
> afraid lest they should only exist as a dead sect, having the
> form of religion without the power. And this undoubtedly
> will be the case unless they hold fast the *doctrine, spirit,*
> and *discipline* with which they first set out.[6]

Our hope is that *A Disciple's Heart* will draw individuals and congregations more deeply into the *doctrine, discipline,* and *spirit* with which the early Methodists first set out.

Our Wesleyan *doctrine* reminds us of who we are and why we are here.

- It's a theology that is centered in the love of God.
- It's a way of discipleship grounded in Wesley's understanding of grace—the relentless love of God that loves us enough to meet us where we are but loves us too much to leave us there.
- It's a process of sanctifying grace in which the Spirit of God is relentlessly at work to form us into the likeness of Christ.
- It's a life of servanthood that sends us into the world, not to condemn the world but to participate in God's transformation of it.

Our *discipline* defines the way we put our beliefs into action. The early Methodists were not as unique in what they believed as they were in the methods by which they practiced it. Their critics called them "Methodists" precisely because they were so "methodical" in their spiritual disciplines. In *A Disciple's Path* we invited participants to practice the spiritual disciplines by which we are formed into people who love God and love others. This resource builds on the foundation of those disciplines to lead followers of Christ into a deeper experience of love and grace. As in *A Disciple's Path*, we draw on the example of Benjamin Ingham, who joined a small group of fellow students at Oxford University in 1729 with John Wesley as their mentor. Ingham's journal provides an intimate look at the life of the first Methodists and will be a guide for us along our way.

If our doctrine reminds us of our mission and our discipline defines our method, then it is the *spirit* of love and grace that energizes us along the journey of discipleship. Wesleyan discipleship is not a self-help guide to a better life. It is an invitation to enter into the spiritual disciplines by which the Holy Spirit does in and through us that which we can never do for or by ourselves. For that reason, *A Disciple's Heart* places a particular emphasis on the work of the Holy Spirit by inviting us into the life of the Trinity.

As you journey through *A Disciple's Heart*, several resources will guide you.

The *Daily Workbook* is designed to help you develop your own pattern of spiritual discipline by providing Scripture and commentary for five days each week. Each day includes reflective questions, meditative prayer practices, and suggestions for action and response.

This *Companion Reader* probes more deeply into each week's subject with biblical, historical, and practical insights that are rooted in the Wesleyan tradition. Whether you are a small group member or group leader, this book is intended to help you dig deeper into the practices that help us to grow in love and grace. Each chapter corresponds to a week of study in the *Daily Workbook* and can be read during the week in preparation for the group session. This book also can be used as a freestanding resource for personal growth as well as preparation for worship, teaching, and preaching when using *A Disciple's Heart* in a church-wide initiative.

A *Leader Guide* is provided for those who are facilitating a small group. An essential part of the Wesleyan tradition is the importance of small group community for spiritual growth, personal accountability, and service to the needs of others modeled after the Holy Club at Oxford. The *Leader Guide* provides a step-by-step process for facilitating a group in which participants share and practice what they are learning in Christian community with other disciples who are walking the same path. In addition, a *Leader Toolkit* (available as a free download and a flash drive in the *Leader Kit*) provides additional leader helps such as reminder e-mails, PowerPoints, and handouts.

It is our prayer that the Spirit of God will use these resources to equip you with practical tools by which the love of God revealed in Jesus transforms your heart into the likeness of Christ.

Shortly after experiencing his heart "strangely warmed" at Aldersgate, John Wesley preached a sermon in which he described the love of God as that which

O for a heart to praise my God,
A heart from sin set free,
A heart that always feels Thy blood
So freely shed for me.

Thy nature, gracious Lord, impart;
Come quickly from above;
Write Thy new name upon my heart,
Thy new, best name of Love.[7]
—Charles Wesley

"engrosses the whole heart, as rakes up all the affections, as fills the entire capacity of the soul." He concluded by challenging the congregation with a question that continues to be at the center of Wesleyan discipleship: "Is the love of God shed abroad in your heart?"[8] It was Wesley's way of asking, "How is your heart?" We will explore that question together in the weeks ahead in the expectation that the same Spirit that warmed the hearts of the early Methodists will warm ours.

1
WHERE DO WE GO FROM HERE?

Our destination was the Hancock Shaker Village in Pittsfield, Massachusetts. The question was how to get there.

My eyes were focused on my iPhone. Our hostess was going by memory, having spent the summer in the Berkshires for many years. My wife had the tourist map in her hands. I kept saying we'd never get there if we kept going the way we were heading. My wife kept insisting that it was straight ahead.

It turned out that she was correct. If they had followed me, we would have gotten somewhere, but it wouldn't have been the place we wanted to be!

Whether we use Google, a printed map, or our intuition, two questions are critical to every trip we take: *Where are we now?* and *Where are we going?* Where we begin determines how we get to where we want to be.

The same principle holds true for the spiritual journey in our relationship with God. The sheer pace of change around us can create a sense of personal and spiritual whiplash. The confusing and sometimes conflicted directional signs that we depended on in the past can leave us wondering if the path we are following in the present will get us where we want to be in the future. The nonstop chatter of the noisy world around us can drown out the deepest voice within us.

We need an inner compass that is fixed on "true north" to guide us through the unexpected twists and turns of our lives—a spiritual GPS to keep us on the right path. For people of biblical faith, the whole story of God's relationship with the creation in Scripture becomes the map we follow. As Christian disciples, we find our "true north" in the words, will, and way of Jesus Christ. His life, death, and resurrection set our course for the abundant life he promised. Like the voice in the GPS that redirects us when we turn in the wrong direction, the

Holy Spirit becomes the inner voice that redirects us when we drift away from the path.

Where the Journey Begins

One of my pastoral mentors liked to say that none of us wants to begin where we are; we would rather begin where we would be if we had started when we should have. But there's no way around it. We have to begin where we are, bringing with us all the doubts, questions, fears, and hopes that emerge out of the experiences that have shaped our lives to that point. Then, somewhere along the way...

- We hear Jesus offer the invitation, "Follow me." Like his first disciples, we may not know where this journey will take us, but we trust that he knows the way better than we do.
- We commit all that we know of ourselves to all that we know of Christ in the confidence that as we get to know both ourselves and the One we are following more deeply, our commitment will continue to grow until the life that became flesh in Jesus becomes a living reality in us.
- We experience God's forgiveness and grace through repentance and begin a new life in Christ by faith.
- We enter into a way of discipleship that is rooted in Scripture and defined by the way, truth, and life revealed in Jesus.
- We are born anew into a community of disciples for whom the cross and the Resurrection become the ongoing metaphor of dying and being raised with Christ.
- We experience the power of the Holy Spirit as we practice the essential disciplines by which we actually become people who love God and love others.
- We become the agents of God's kingdom becoming a tangible reality in this world.
- We look forward with confident hope to the fulfillment of God's saving purpose when God's kingdom comes and God's will is done on earth as it is in heaven.

In his own spiritual journey, Benjamin Ingham was searching for practical direction in living the holy life when he made his way to John Wesley's apartment in the spring of 1734. John Robson joined them for breakfast, during which Wesley recommended that Ingham and Robson begin meeting together once a week to study Scripture, to encourage each other's faith, to hold each other accountable to their spiritual disciplines, and to serve the needs of the poor. He also taught them to keep a daily journal of their discipleship.[2]

> **"In a higher world it is otherwise, but here below to live is to change, and to be perfect is to have changed often."**[1]
> —Cardinal John Newman

The experience of those students became the starting point for a spiritual awakening that swept across England and launched a movement that would lead to ministry and mission around the globe. But it all began in the hearts of a few people who longed for a deeper, more transformative relationship with Jesus Christ.

My discipleship journey began before I can remember. Like John Wesley, who was nurtured in the faith by his parents, and Timothy, who received the faith from his mother and grandmother (2 Timothy 1:5-6), I was born into a deeply committed Christian home with parents who encouraged my childhood faith. While there were many times in different places when I responded to the invitation to follow Christ, some of the most formative were at summer youth camp. Each evening we would hike up a grass-covered, central Pennsylvania hillside called Vesper Hill for evening worship. I don't remember a word that was preached, but I remember the way each service ended. After a time of silent reflection, we would fold up our blankets and hike back down the hill, singing, "Follow, I will follow Thee, my Lord, / Follow ev'ry passing day."[3]

I've been following him ever since.

I've discovered that every disciple has a unique story of the way his or her journey began. There is no one-size-fits-all pattern. Though some stories are similar, none is quite the same as any other. They are not unlike the unique stories married couples tell about how they met and fell in love. The evidence is that the Spirit of God is amazingly patient and infinitely creative in finding ways to enter into our lives and call us into the life of discipleship.

This should not come as a surprise. Look at the amazing variety of ways people in the New Testament experienced Christ:

- Shepherds heard the good news in the blazing light of angels.
- Wise men found the Christ child at the end of a long and arduous search.
- Fishermen met Jesus while working their nets.
- Nathaniel discovered that Jesus knew him long before he knew Jesus.
- Matthew met Jesus while collecting taxes, and a house full of tax collectors and sinners met Jesus at a dinner party in Matthew's house.
- Mary and Martha encountered him in the comfort of their home.
- A centurion at the cross realized that Jesus is the Son of God by watching him die.
- Mary Magdalene mistook him for a gardener at the tomb.
- Saul was blinded by his presence on the Damascus Road.
- Timothy learned of Christ from his mother and grandmother.

The gospel is the story of how ordinary people in ordinary places discovered the extraordinary presence of Jesus and rose up to follow him.

For Albert Schweitzer (1875–1965), following Jesus meant leaving a career as a musician, theologian, and philosopher to serve as a medical doctor in Africa. Here's the way he described the discovery:

> He comes to us as One unknown, without a name, as of old, by the lake-side, He came to those men who knew Him not. He speaks to us the same word: "Follow thou me!" and sets us to the tasks which He has to fulfill for our time. He commands. And to those who obey Him, whether they be wise or simple, He will reveal Himself in the toils, the conflicts, the sufferings which they shall pass through in His fellowship, and, as an ineffable mystery, they shall learn in their own experience Who He is.[4]

Wherever you are in your spiritual journey, continued growth in love and grace involves naming where you are along the pathway of discipleship:

- Where did your discipleship journey begin?
- Where are you now?
- What is the next appropriate step in your discipleship?

What's Your Destination?

If that's where the journey begins, the next question is where the journey is going. What is the destination?

The destination of Christian discipleship in the Wesleyan tradition is nothing less than a spiritual heart transplant. It is the fulfillment of the promise that came from God to the Old Testament prophet Ezekiel:

> *I will give you a new heart and put a new spirit in you. I will remove your stony heart from your body and replace it with a living one. (Ezekiel 36:26)*

Ezekiel caught the vision of an inner transformation that goes far beyond external behaviors and involves the transformation of the inner core of a human life. But the reality is that often it is much easier to focus attention on obeying rules than on experiencing transformation.

In the case of Jesus' first disciples, it was their lack of appropriate table manners that drove the Pharisees crazy. When they saw Jesus' disciples eating without washing their hands, they went ballistic. They asked, "Why are your disciples not living according to the rules handed down by the elders but instead eat food with ritually unclean hands?" (Mark 7:5).

Jesus turned on them with words from the prophet Isaiah: "This people honors me with their lips, / but their hearts are far away from me" (Mark 7:6). He told the crowd, "Nothing outside of a person can enter and contaminate a person in God's sight; rather, the things that come out of a person contaminate the person" (Mark 7:14-15). He made his point with a graphic illustration of the human body to say that "It is what comes out of a person that defiles. For it is from within, from the human heart, that evil intentions come" (Mark 7:20-21 NRSV).

> "By Methodists I mean, a people who profess to pursue (in whatsoever measure they have attained) holiness of heart and life, inward and outward conformity in all things to the revealed will of God... in justice, mercy, and truth, or universal love filling the heart, and governing the life."[5]
> —John Wesley

Jesus did not come with a new set of rules to control us from the outside in. Rather, he came to call us to a way of living that transforms us from the inside out. The critical factor is not how perfectly we live by the rules but how deeply

17

we love from the heart. For Jesus, the heart of the matter is always a matter of the heart. Wesley called the process of heart transformation "Christian perfection," "sanctification," or "being made perfect in love." The early Methodists named this spiritual destination "holiness of heart and life."

Going On to Perfection

John Wesley asked his preachers the same questions more than two hundred years ago, but hearing Bishop Joel McDavid ask the questions at my ordination ceremony in his resonate voice with a slow, Southern drawl made them an unforgettable part of my life. Four decades later, they still lure me toward a goal I have not yet reached:

> Are you going on to perfection?
> Do you expect to be made perfect in love in this life?
> Are you earnestly striving after perfection in love?[6]

I agree with Kathleen Norris who called *perfectionism* "one of the scariest words I know."[7] But as she went on to say, "To 'be perfect,' in the sense that Jesus means it, is to make room for growth, for the changes that bring us to maturity, to ripeness."[8]

Perfection in the biblical sense is the end or goal toward which all things are moving. It is what our world and our lives will look like when God's saving purpose is fully accomplished. It is the fulfillment of the prayer that God's kingdom come and God's will be done on earth—in us—as it is in heaven.

Richard Heitzenrater, who discovered Benjamin Ingham's diary in 1969 in the Methodist Archives in London, said that for the Oxford Methodists, the goal of Christian perfection was not to act perfectly but rather "to *be* perfect, to achieve an inward perfection of intentions and attitudes, of will as well as of understanding."[9] As Paul Wesley Chilcote defined it, sanctification (Christian perfection) is "that process by which the Spirit makes us more and more like Jesus."[10]

Wesley found the idea of Christian perfection in the Scriptures as well as the spiritual tradition that goes back to the early church fathers. A twentieth-century Roman Catholic monk named Thomas Merton found it in the writings of Saint Chrysostom. In the fourth century, Chrysostom rejected the assumption that "monks alone need to strive for perfection, while lay people need only avoid hell." Chrysostom said that "both lay people and monks have to lead a very positive and constructive Christian life."[11]

Benjamin Ingham's diary demonstrates the intensity with which the Oxford Methodists held themselves accountable for even the most minute behaviors that would either help or hinder their pursuit of holiness. Their shared discipline is a reminder that growth in holiness results from a combination of receptivity to the work of the Holy Spirit and disciplined action that brings our lives into harmony with the holiness we seek. It is the combination of belief and action that results in transformation.

> "Love is the fulfilling of the law, the end of the commandment. ... In this is perfection, and glory, and happiness. The one perfect good shall be your one ultimate end. ... In every step you take, be this the glorious point that terminates your view."[12]
> —John Wesley

A Centering Way of Life

In the *Daily Workbook*, we define Christian perfection as "an end without an ending." It's the end toward which all things are moving, the fulfillment of God's saving purpose in our lives and in the whole creation. We touch on the same idea in *A Disciple's Path* when we define a disciple as "a follower of Jesus Christ whose life is *centering* on loving God and loving others." The continuous present tense of the word "centering" indicates an ongoing process by which the Spirit of God is persistently at work to accomplish God's loving purpose in and through our lives. Eugene Peterson used the same word when warning us that "Americans in general have little tolerance for a *centering way of life* that is submissive to the condition in which growth takes place" (emphasis added).[13]

Peterson is onto something. Our culture prefers a quick fix for everything. We don't have much patience with the slow and sometimes tedious disciplines by which lasting change or growth takes place. But the transformation of the human heart doesn't happen overnight. Sanctification, the journey toward Christian perfection, takes time. It's like the old adage that if God wants a mushroom, he can pop it up overnight; but if God wants to grow a sequoia, it's going to take some time. A person can decide to follow Jesus in a moment, but being formed into Christ's likeness takes a lifetime. We can catch a glimpse of the kingdom of God in a brief parable, but working it out in this world takes time and costly effort. Christian perfection is the result of the patient, persistent work of the Spirit of God within and through us.

Pastoral colleague Magrey R. deVega gave me a fresh way of imagining the process of sanctification when he reflected on a visit to Mount Rushmore. After viewing the breathtaking spectacle of Gutzon Borglum's carvings of the four presidents, he stopped by the gift shop where he purchased a photograph of the mountain taken in 1902 before the sculptor began his work. (You can find this picture on the Internet.) That photograph now hangs in Magrey's office as a reminder of what he describes as the way the Spirit "patiently, diligently carves away at the hardened facades that conceal the image of God that lies deep within us."[14]

What is our calling's glorious hope,
But inward holiness?
For this to Jesus I look up;
I calmly wait for this.

When Jesus makes my heart His home,
My sin shall all depart;
And lo! He saith, I quickly come,
To fill and rule thy heart.

Be it according to Thy Word;
Redeem me from all sin;
My heart would now receive Thee, Lord,
Come in, my Lord, come in![15]
—Charles Wesley

It took Borglum twelve years to carve away the stone in order to reveal all the faces that he alone could see inside the mountain. This could be a metaphor for the way God sees something within each of us that no one else can see. The new discovery for Magrey was that Borglum allowed an extra three inches in each of the figures' features to account for the weather, which wears away an inch of granite every one hundred thousand years. This suggests that it will take three hundred thousand years for the carving to actually fulfill the sculptor's intention. Magrey wrote:

> I can see that at every turn, God has been at work,
> chipping away at our hardened hearts and rough-edged
> personalities, teaching us—sometimes painfully—
> about being utterly dependent on God and clear in our
> commitment to God's ways. Just like Borglum's crew used
> both explosives and nail files to carve into the granite, our

lives are filled with monumental moments, both great and
small, that change our lives forever.[16]

As followers of Christ, we are always works in progress; imperfect disciples on the way toward perfection; ordinary men and women who need the
continuing work of the Divine Cardiologist to heal our stony hearts, replacing
them with hearts that are fully alive and being formed into a human likeness of
the heart of God. By God's grace, we are going on to perfection.

2
WALKING THE WAY OF SALVATION

In January 1733, Benjamin Ingham recorded, "[I] am resolved, God's grace assisting me, to make the salvation of my soul my chief and only concern but never to depend upon my own strength because I can do nothing without God's assistance."[1] His resolution raises some formative questions for us.

- What do we mean by *salvation*?
- How do we experience it?
- Who can be saved?

Whatever Became of Sin?

We can't experience salvation without facing up to the reality of sin. But even the word sin *may* be harder to find these days.

Sin was among a variety of words rooted in the Christian tradition that were removed from the most recent edition of *Oxford Junior Dictionary*, along with *altar, disciple, pew,* and *saint*. The editors explained the exclusion by saying that "the dictionary needs to evolve to reflect the fact that Britain has become a modern, multicultural, multi-faith society." They said the decisions were made in part by looking at the numbers of times the excluded words appeared in current children's literature.[2]

Before criticizing the British publishers, it might be helpful to ask when was the last time you heard someone acknowledge that he or she had sinned. When a public figure is caught in some inappropriate or illegal behavior, the typical pattern is to shift into the passive voice by saying, "Mistakes were made"—rather than taking personal responsibility for their actions. The traditional Prayer of Confession has largely been removed from our worship liturgy as a relic of a more penitential past in a desire to offer a more positive view of the faith. The word *sin* has largely drifted out of our consciousness or has been consigned to self-righteous preachers who are quick to attack other people's sins.

Whatever became of sin? Karl Menninger asked that question in his book by that title. The world-renowned psychiatrist rattled the cage of our self-affirming complacency when he declared that "sin is still with us, by us, and in us."[3] With clinical accuracy, he described the ways we are affected by the "willful, defiant, or disloyal quality" of sin, which he defined as "a refusal of the love of others."[4]

Menninger's answer to the question is still accurate today. Just because we avoid the word doesn't mean that sin no longer exists. We may not feel the same level of guilt for sin that motivated earlier generations to come to worship with an all-pervasive fear of God's wrath, but when we look behind the suffering and conflict of our time, we see all too clearly the sins of insatiable greed, racial prejudice, ethnic bigotry, economic injustice, unrestrained lust, and self-serving anger. When we look deeply inside our own hardened hearts, we can name the ways in which our lives are out of line with God's best intentions for us—the ways we hurt ourselves and one another because of our radical self-absorption. In our heart of hearts, we know that "all have sinned and fall short of God's glory" (Romans 3:23).

> "Salvation is God not only reaching out but also specifically reaching down. Jesus makes friends in low places....Salvation is Jesus getting down on our level, so that we might rise to his."[5]
> —William H. Willimon

Thomas Merton diagnosed the cause of our hard hearts when he defined sin as "the rejection of the inner order and peace that comes from our union with the divine will...our refusal to be what we were created to be—sons [and daughters] of God."[6] We know there are ways in which we need salvation. And we know that it is not something we can create or manage on our own.

Making Things Right

In every word processing software program there is an icon or command for adjusting the lines on the page to fit evenly within the margins on both sides of the screen. In the printing business, that is called justification. It means that all the words on the page are realigned so that they are in right relationship with each other within the margins on the page.

The Apostle Paul never could have imagined a computer screen, but the metaphor of page justification is not far from what he was talking about in the letter to the Romans when he said that we are "justified by faith" (Romans 5:1 NRSV). Justification is the way God realigns our lives to bring us into right relationship with God's saving purpose for our lives and for this world. It's the way God makes things right. It's God's work of salvation.

John Wesley knew the Bible; he understood the meaning of the words. He studied theology at Oxford and was ordained as a priest in the Church of England. But despite all of that, he still wrestled with a penetrating awareness of his own sin and a relentless insecurity about his own relationship with God.

While serving as a missionary in Georgia, Wesley confessed, "I went to America to convert the Indians, but, O! who shall convert me?"[7] Not long after returning to England, he reluctantly went to a small group meeting at Aldersgate Street on May 24, 1738. Here's the way he described what happened as he listened to someone read from Luther's Preface to the Romans.

> About a quarter before nine, while he was describing the
> change which God works in the heart through faith in
> Christ, I felt my heart strangely warmed. I felt I did trust
> in Christ, Christ alone, for salvation; and an assurance
> was given me that He had taken away my sins, even mine,
> and saved me from the law of sin and death.[8]

Don't miss the relational language of Wesley's witness. In the Wesleyan tradition, salvation is not a legalistic contract or judicial change of status but a profoundly personal change in our relationship with God.

Historians and theologians sometimes debate the significance of what happened at Aldersgate, but it would be hard to miss the experiential power of it. The things Wesley believed in his head became a living reality in his heart. He received the inner assurance of salvation—that God had forgiven his sins and brought him into right relationship with God. He would spend the rest of his life proclaiming to others that they could experience the same assurance of salvation. John's brother Charles had a similar experience of grace and described the essence of salvation when he wrote these words:

And can it be that I should gain
An interest in the Savior's blood!
Died he for me? who caused his pain!
For me? who him to death pursued?
Amazing love! How can it be
That thou, my God, shouldst die for me?...

Long my imprisoned spirit lay,
Fast bound in sin and nature's night;
Thine eye diffused a quickening ray;
I woke, the dungeon flamed with light;
My chains fell off, my heart was free,
I rose, went forth, and followed thee.[9]

At the center of the Wesleyan understanding of salvation is the heart-level assurance of God's saving grace that meets us wherever we are, forgives what we have been, and continuously works within us to enable us to become all that God intends us to be. From beginning to end, it is a work of grace.

Washed in the Water of Grace

One of the basic biblical metaphors for salvation is being washed, cleansed, or made clean. Sin always leaves us feeling unclean. We hear it in David's prayer after his affair with Bathsheba and his murder of her husband, Uriah:

> *Purify me with hyssop and I will be clean;*
> *wash me and I will be whiter than snow...*
> *Hide your face from my sins;*
> *wipe away all my guilty deeds!*
> *Create a clean heart for me, God;*
> *put a new, faithful spirit deep inside me! (Psalm 51:7, 9-10)*

Naaman is another biblical example. He was the military commander for the king of Aram. He was a Gentile, someone who was outside the boundaries of the Covenant. He had wealth, position, and power. But behind that impressive facade, he "suffered from leprosy" (2 Kings 5:1 NRSV).

In the Bible, "leprosy" refers to a broad assortment of skin diseases, not just the one we know as Hansen's disease. All were thought to be contagious, which is why lepers were considered ritually unclean. They were separated from the community, cut off from their family and friends, excluded from the Temple, and forced to survive in total isolation from everyone around them.

The fact that he was a leper was the dark secret Naaman kept hidden as long as possible. When Naaman had nowhere else to turn, he came to the prophet Elisha with a camel train loaded down with gifts and a letter from his king, all intended to make a big impression on the prophet. But Elisha didn't even come out to meet him. He sent a messenger to tell Naaman that if he would wash in the Jordan seven times, he would be clean.

Naaman was insulted and incensed, but one of his servants suggested that if the prophet had asked him to do something difficult, he probably would have done it. So why not give washing in the Jordan a try?

The text says, "Naaman went down..." (2 Kings 5:14). I suspect the Hebrew storytellers were describing more in that phrase than mere geography. He stepped down from his place of authority. He lowered himself to the humiliating instructions from the prophet. He went down into the Jordan River seven times. When he came up from the water, "his skin was restored like that of a young boy" (2 Kings 5:14).

Naaman returned to Elisa and said, "Now I know for certain that there's no God anywhere on earth except in Israel" (2 Kings 5:15). By the unearned, undeserved, unexpected grace of God, he had been made clean.

Jesus' reference to this story underscores just how offensive God's expansive grace can seem to religious people who believe that they have a priority claim on God's love. In his first sermon in his hometown, Jesus reminded the faithful Jewish people in the synagogue that "there were also many persons with skin diseases in Israel during the time of the prophet Elisha, but none of them were cleansed. Instead, Naaman the Syrian was cleansed" (see Luke 4:27). The reminder of the outrageously inclusive grace of God made Jesus' hometown crowd so angry that they ran him out of town (Luke 4:29).

The spirit of Naaman may be lurking in the background of the story of John the Baptist, who showed up along the same Jordan River "calling for people to be baptized to show that they were changing their hearts and lives and wanted God to forgive their sins" (Luke 3:3). The same water of God's cleansing grace that washed over Naaman continues to wash over us in the sacrament of baptism.

Remember Your Baptism

If you were a new follower of Christ in the first or second century, you would have prepared for baptism throughout Lent. On the night before Easter, with the men and women separated, you would strip off your old clothing and be led into the baptismal waters as naked as the day you were born. Women were instructed to let their hair down and lay aside any jewelry.[10] You would go under the water as a symbol of dying with Christ. When you came up out of the water, you would be wrapped in a new, white robe and walk into the light of resurrection morning as a new person, washed clean in the grace of God.

While there is some debate about the actual practice of naked baptism in the early church, it is a powerful visual image of the analogy Paul used when he told the Colossians to strip off the dirty clothes of their old ways of living and put on the new clothes of their life in Christ (Colossians 3:1-17 NRSV).

> "In baptism we are clothed, once and for all, with a forgiveness woven for us by Jesus' death and resurrection. The grace of baptism, therefore, is quite fittingly referred to as *habitual* grace (from 'habit' as in 'a nun's habit') because we wear it, all our lives long as an irremovable vestment of forgiveness."[11]
> —Robert Farrar Capon

I've forgotten the woman's name, but I have never forgotten her face. I had never met her before she came to the church office looking for a pastor. With naked honesty, she dumped her story out before me the way a person dumps dirty laundry on the floor. She never looked me in the eye but stared down at the floor as if she could see it all piled there before us.

I listened. I prayed for her. Then, without being prompted, she prayed and confessed it all to God. When she finished her prayer, I spoke the words of assurance, "If we confess our sins, he is faithful and just to forgive us our sins and cleanse us from everything we've done wrong" (1 John 1:9). She lifted her head, looked me in the eye, and with tears of joy running down her cheeks, she smiled as she said, "I feel clean!"

In the Wesleyan tradition, we do not re-baptize. But we do believe that the grace we affirm in waters of baptism is the free-flowing river of salvation that continues to wash away our sin the whole way along our discipleship journey.

Many congregations celebrate The Reaffirmation of Baptism at the beginning of each year when the liturgical calendar remembers the Baptism of our Lord. Throughout my years as a pastor I stood beside the baptismal font each year and watched as people came to the water. Some touched the water to their foreheads; some let the water flow through their fingers; some helped their children reach out to touch the water. It was always a stirring witness to the power of this tangible sign of the intangible grace of God.

One year, after touching the water, a man stepped over to me, wrapped his arm around me, and said, "I remember when you baptized me!"

I confess that I had forgotten the day I baptized him. But he had not forgotten. And neither had God. It was the beginning of this man's journey along the way of salvation.

The Way of Salvation

In his sermon "On Working Out Our Own Salvation," Wesley described the spiritual journey of salvation. It begins in "preventing" or "prevenient" grace. The Spirit of God plants within us an initial awareness of our sin and the hunger for God's grace, which leads us toward what Wesley called "convincing" or "converting" grace. It may be experienced in a multitude of ways, but it always includes repentance, a turning away from sin and a turning toward God. This begins the process of "sanctifying" grace, the ongoing work of the Spirit by which we are formed into the likeness of Christ. Along the way there are decisive moments of continuous growth in which love increases "till we all come to... the measure of the stature of the fullness of Christ" (Ephesians 4:13 NKJV).

> "Conversion is not a date to be remembered (although 'the hour I first believed' is holy) so much as it is a launch to be celebrated from that day forward."[12]
> —Steve Harper

Conversion is one of the words we use to describe the transformation that happens in the human heart as we experience salvation. In computer technology, conversion is the process of shifting from one operating system platform to another that fundamentally changes the way the system works. In the same way, God's work of salvation shifts the fundamental operating system of our lives—our hearts—from a life that is centered in ourselves to a life that is centering in loving God and loving others. All of it is an underserved, unearned gift of God's grace.

Grace for All

Although every Christian denomination proclaims God's grace, different denominations have at different times proclaimed that grace in very different ways.

Two centuries separated John Calvin (1509–1564) and John Wesley (1703–1791), but the theological debate between them continues to this day. That debate found human expression in the relationship between John Wesley and George Whitefield (1714–1770).

Charles Wesley invited Whitefield to join the Holy Club at Oxford. John Wesley showed Whitefield the importance of small group community and the focus on holy living. Whitefield convinced Wesley of the effectiveness of outdoor preaching, which marked a radical shift in Wesley's life and ministry. Together they gave energetic leadership to the spiritual awakening that was spreading across England.

While Wesley and Whitefield agreed on most things, the breach in their partnership came around Whitefield's preaching of Calvin's doctrine of *predestination*, the belief that God has chosen in advance who will be saved and who will be lost. This ran directly against the grain of Wesley's understanding of the universal love of God and the invitation to anyone and everyone to experience God's forgiveness and grace.

In 1740, John Wesley published a scathing critique of predestination in his sermon on "Free Grace." He declared, "The grace or love of God, whence cometh our salvation, is FREE IN ALL, and FREE FOR ALL." He went on to offer "plain proof that the doctrine of predestination is not a doctrine of God."[13]

Aware of the damage the sermon would do to his friendship with Whitefield, Wesley prefaced the sermon by saying, "Nothing but the strongest conviction...could have induced me openly to oppose the sentiments of those whom I esteem for their work's sake: At whose feet may I be found in the day of the Lord Jesus!" He requested that any response to the sermon be done "in love, and in the spirit of meekness . . . that even according to this time it may be said, 'See how these Christians love one another!' "[14]

The debate continued, with Wesley and Whitefield leading separate branches of the revival. While never denying their differences, they honored each other's ministry. Over time, their friendship was restored. In 1755, Charles Wesley wrote, "Come on, my Whitefield! (since the strife is past) / And friends at first are friends again at last."[15] Whitfield requested that John Wesley preach at his funeral, which Wesley did in 1770. But the theological differences that divided them continue to separate the Wesleyan and Calvinist branches on the Christian family tree today.

Charles Wesley proclaimed the Wesleyan belief in the universal love of God when he wrote:

> Come, sinners, to the gospel feast;
> Let every soul be Jesus' guest.
> Ye need not one be left behind,
> For God hath bid all humankind.[16]

I keep in my files an advertisement for British Airways that appeared during the celebration of the United States bicentennial in 1976. The portly British actor Robert Morley, wearing a bowler hat and holding a small American flag, looks out at us with a reassuring face above the caption that reads, "Come home, America, all is forgiven."

That's similar to the spirit in which God invites everyone to come home through his grace.

- We come as sinners who need to be washed in the water of God's forgiveness.
- We come as strangers invited to a banquet of salvation we neither earned nor deserved.
- We come as hungry disciples to receive nourishment for our journey.
- We come as imperfect people who see in the water of baptism and the bread and cup of Communion the perfect love of God.
- We are bathed in the water of grace.
- We are nourished with the bread of life.
- We are saved.

Wherever our discipleship begins, Wesley's understanding of salvation describes the way God's grace meets us where we are and begins the work of transformation in our hearts that leads us along the journey toward perfection. As E. Stanley Jones remarked about his own salvation, we are always "Christians-in-the-making."[17]

3
BY THE POWER OF THE SPIRIT

Wesleyan discipleship is an invitation to enter into the spiritual disciplines by which the Holy Spirit does in and through us that which we can never do for or by ourselves. It is the Spirit that transforms our hearts and shapes us into the image of Christ. For that reason, *A Disciple's Heart* places a particular emphasis on the work of the Holy Spirit by inviting us into the life of the Trinity.

The Trinity can be a challenging concept to explain. One of my colleagues says that the problem with the Trinity is that if you don't believe it you lose your soul, but if you try to explain it you lose your mind.

Eugene Peterson pointed us in the right direction when he wrote, "Trinity has nothing to do with arithmetic." He went on to say that belief in the Trinity is not "puzzling over how one equals three or three equals one . . . Trinity is the church's way of learning to think and respond relationally to God as he reveals himself to us as Father, Son, and Holy Spirit."[1]

One year I was wrestling with how to explain the Trinity in a sermon for Trinity Sunday—the Sunday after Pentecost—when I discovered the *Untermyer Fountain* (also known as *Three Dancing Maidens*) in Central Park, New York City. (You can find a picture of the fountain on the Internet.) There's no reason to assume that the sculptor had Trinitarian theology in mind when he designed the original bronze in Germany, but the image of a vibrant, never-ending dance of life and love opened a new way of experiencing the Trinity in my own life even as it provided a theme for my sermon.

I didn't know that a friend halfway across the country would use the same metaphor for his sermon that Sunday. Magrey deVega was playing the role of the king in a community theater production of the Rogers and Hammerstein musical *The King and I*. In the pivotal scene, the king asks Anna, "Shall we dance?" She agrees to teach him. He is clumsy at first, but by the time the curtain falls, they are sailing around the stage in a glorious waltz that is the first expression of their love for each other.

Magrey's congregation laughed at his description of his first attempt at the dance scene. He compared himself to Jabba the Hutt in *Return of the Jedi*, thumping his tail and waving his arms in jerky, awkward movements. A few rehearsals later, his daughter told him that he was starting to look less like a walrus. Finally, after weeks of rehearsal, he was able to glide across the stage in the climactic scene.

He went on to say that his foray into the world of dance had given him a new appreciation for dance as a metaphor to describe the Trinity:

> The Father, the Son, and the Holy Spirit work separately
> but simultaneously as one movement, one free-flowing
> energy of divine love. It is one dance, with three dancers,
> all in such perfect synchronicity that their separateness
> is indistinguishable from the other. . . . It begins with the
> relationships that God maintains within the Godhead,
> and it extends outwardly, inviting all of creation to take
> part of that dance. . . . So, . . . Shall We Dance?[2]

Imagining the Trinity as a dance was not an original idea for either my pastor friend or me. In fact, it goes back to a fourth-century archbishop named Gregory of Nazianzus, who described the Trinity with the word *perichoresis*. It comes from two Greek words: *peri*, which means "around," and *chorein*, which means "to make room" or "give way."[3] In classical Greek the word is *choreia*, meaning "choral dance."[4]

C. S. Lewis used the same image when he wrote: "In Christianity God is not a static thing . . . but a dynamic, pulsating activity . . . a kind of dance."[5]

More recently, Paul Young got to the point of the metaphor in *The Shack* when Papa, the first person of the Trinity, explained, "We are in a circle of relationship, not a chain of command . . . What you're seeing here is relationship without any overlay of power."[6] Papa invites the broken-hearted Mack to come into the dance: "We want to share with you the love and joy and freedom and light that we already know within ourself. We created you . . . to be in face-to-face relationship with us, to join our circle of love."[7]

The mistake well-intended preachers often make on Trinity Sunday is to attempt to explain the Trinity when our purpose in worship is to celebrate and experience it. Academicians can bend their brains with historical, biblical, and theological debates, all of which have their place. But for growing disciples who are on their way to perfection, the invitation is for each of us to join the living, pulsating, dancing circle of the Father, Son, and Holy Spirit as we exclaim:

> Holy, holy holy! Lord God Almighty!...
> God in three persons, blessed Trinity![8]

Radical Renovation

So, what would it look like for us to join the dance of the Trinity? How can we imagine the difference the Holy Spirit actually makes in our lives?

When the New Amsterdam Theater opened in New York City in 1903, it was one of the most magnificent theaters in the country. In its heyday it was home for the Ziegfeld Follies. George M. Cohan, Eddie Cantor, and Fred Astaire sang and danced their way across its stage. But after the Depression, it fell on hard times. When its doors closed in 1981, it was a decrepit movie house where inebriated street people slept through X-rated films.

For the sake of historical preservation, the state and city took ownership of the property, but the building continued to decay for more than a decade until the Disney Corporation took control.

A friend who worked on the project told me that what they found was even worse than they expected. Years of abuse and neglect had left the roof leaking, beams rotting, and the plaster falling from the walls. They brought in their best people and their almost inexhaustible resources and went to work. A couple of years and over $30 million later, the theater was not only restored to its former grandeur but also technologically equipped for the next century. The fundamental change for the New Amsterdam Theater came because it was taken over by a new resident who did a total renovation of the theater from the inside out to give it new life for the future.

I remembered that story when I came to this passage in the J.B. Phillips' paraphrase of Paul's letter to the Ephesians:

I pray that out of the glorious richness of his resources he will enable you to know the strength of the spirit's inner re-inforcement—that Christ may actually live in your hearts by your faith. And I pray that you, firmly fixed in love yourselves, may be able to grasp (with all Christians) how wide and deep and long and high is the love of Christ—and to know for yourselves that love so far beyond our comprehension. May you be filled though all your being with God himself! (Ephesians 3:16-19 JBP)

O that the Comforter would come,
Nor visit as a transient guest;
But fix in me His constant home,
And take possession of my breast,
And fix in me His loved abode,
The temple of indwelling God![9]
–Charles Wesley

Paul describes God's work in our hearts as nothing less than a total renovation project in which the Holy Spirit moves in to reinforce that which is good and to restore that which is damaged. The holy life Benjamin Ingham and the early Methodists were seeking is nothing less than a redesign of our desires and a remodeling of our ambitions from the inside out so that the risen Christ can take up residence in our hearts until we are "filled entirely with the fullness of God" (Ephesians 3:19).

We hear Paul's words as good news. Within every human heart there is a hunger that only God can fill. The deepest truth of our existence is that each of us has a deep longing to know, feel, and sense the presence of God within us. That's not a uniquely Christian thing; it's a human thing. That's who we are as men and women created in the image of God.

We also know the ways that our hearts and lives are like an old building that has been damaged by abuse, neglect, and sin:

- Our neglect of the spiritual disciplines of prayer, Bible study, and worship has left rotting foundations that need to be repaired.
- Our lives are cluttered with the debris of destructive habits, painful memories, damaged emotions, and bitter hurts from the past.
- We have secret closets of greed that need to be opened to the needs of others.
- We board up the windows, lock the doors, and put up fences around the property so that our lives are protected from the pain, suffering, injustice, and conflict of the world around us.

- Our heart, the center room of our personality, is under the control of a self-centered, self-serving, self-deifying form of sin.

The good news of the gospel is that out of the inexhaustible resources of God's love and grace, the Spirit comes to do the inner work of heart renovation that prepares a place for Christ to come, not as a visitor or passing acquaintance but as the One who fills our whole being with the life, love, and power that are alive in the Trinity.

While one part of us receives this word as good news, there is another part of us that isn't quite so sure. If we allow the Spirit to begin the renovation in our lives, then God only knows the kind of changes he might bring.

C. S. Lewis invited us to picture our life as a house. We know we need some obvious repairs—fixing the broken plumbing and repairing the leaking roof. But then God begins making bigger changes that we don't quite understand, some of which are downright painful. God starts knocking out a wall here and putting up a tower there. The Spirit opens our lives to new relationships and possibilities that we never imagined. Lewis wrote, "You thought you were going to be made into a decent little cottage; but He is building a palace. He intends to come and live in it Himself."[10]

Though the changes may be unwanted and uncomfortable, if our goal is to be made perfect in love, if our lives are centering in loving God and loving others, and if the contractor in charge of the renovations is none other than the Spirit of God revealed to us in Jesus Christ, then we know that the changes are for our good and for God's glory. We dare to believe that they are custom-designed to bring out the best within us and to equip us to be the agents of God's love in this world. We know that our only hope for reaching our full potential is to allow the Spirit to clean out the trash, stretch the narrow confines of our human personalities, tear down the walls we have built to protect ourselves, and rebuild our lives into the likeness of Christ until the boundaries of our hearts are defined by the height, breadth, length, and width of the love of God.

Under New Management

Before becoming a follower of Christ, Augustine (A.D. 354–430) lived a hedonistic, self-absorbed life. He was like a lot of folks in our world today—a successful young man with exceptional gifts and talents living in a culture that one of my young adult friends defined as "soulless." My friend said that most of the people with whom he lives and works are having a great time enjoying the stuff that fills their successful, affluent lives. But when you listen deeply to their stories, you discover that many of them are empty or hollow, without any sense of why they are here or what they are expected to do with all that they have.

This emptiness led Augustine to pray, "The house of my soul is too small for you to enter: make it more spacious by your coming. It lies in ruins: rebuild it."[11]

The question is: How are we engaged in this renovation project?

The first step is to recognize our need. The project begins with ruthless honesty as we acknowledge to God and to ourselves our desperate need for God to begin a transforming work in our lives. We might refer to this as a moral inventory.

The second step is to allow the Holy Spirit to enter into our lives and do the work that only the Spirit can do. We claim the promise of the Risen Christ, "Look! I'm standing at the door and knocking. If any hear my voice and open the door, I will come in" (Revelation 3:20).

The third and most difficult step goes on for a lifetime as we learn to surrender—to relinquish control of our lives so that the Spirit can shape, direct, and saturate every part of our existence with the love of God. Benjamin Ingham bore witness to that kind of surrender on Good Friday, 1734, when he wrote, "I did, with all the devotion of my heart and soul, make an entire surrender and resignation of myself and all things belonging to me to Almighty God . . . that he should have the full guiding and governing . . . of me and mine forever."[12]

I have a friend who, like Ingham, was a student at a prestigious university. He was a world-class swimmer on his way to the Olympics when asthma suddenly ended his swimming career. Four years later he wrote to me:

> Asthma left me sad, frustrated, and angry, especially when
> I realized it was going to be with me for the long haul.
> All of my ultimate dreams and goals for swimming were
> shattered during that season, which required me to hang
> up my Speedo forever. To this day, not an afternoon goes
> by that I don't daydream about what might have been.
>
> On one hand I dream about what might have happened
> and wish for that glory. But on the other hand I *know* that
> if I had not gotten sick I would not be in seminary today.
> I don't believe God sent the asthma, but he definitely used

it to bring about his glory. I'm glad that God has more control than I do. If my life were left up to me, I would be in a mess for sure.

My friend relinquished control of his life and future to God. Through the disruption of his plans, he heard the Risen Christ knocking at the door of his life and opened the door to let him in. He completed seminary, had an effective ministry as the pastor of a local church, earned a PhD in Wesleyan theology, and now is a seminary professor training a new generation of pastors. He would say that when you allow the Spirit to begin the work of renovation in your life, you never know where you might end up; but you can be sure it will be better than anything you had planned.

> O, grant that nothing in my soul
> May dwell, but thy pure love alone!
> O may Thy love possess me whole,
> My joy, my treasure, and my crown.
> Strange flames far from my soul remove;
> My every act, word, thought, be love![13]
> —Paul Gerhardt,
>   translated by John Wesley

Are you ready to relinquish control of your life and future to God? Here is an imaginative exercise that can help you to experience the inner renovation of the Spirit of God. Find a solitary place and a quiet time in which you can focus your attention on each of these steps without being in a hurry. Calm yourself in God's presence and ask the Holy Spirit to walk with you. You may wish to journal your responses along the way. My hope is that you will experience the inner reinforcement of the Spirit as you allow the Risen Christ to meet you in each of these places. You may want to share your experience with other members of your small group.

I invite you to:

- Imagine your heart as a house that is customized just for you. Each of our imaginary houses will be very different from the people around us. Picture your house as clearly as you can.
- Imagine that you hear a knock at the door. You recognize the person to be Jesus, and you open the door to let him come in.
- Imagine that Jesus begins to walk through your house, asking you to give him the key to each of the doors.

- He asks for the key to the living room, that public place where you relate to other people, so that his love will flow through you to every person you meet.
- He asks for the key to the study, the room of your intellect, so that his truth can invigorate everything you see, think, or imagine.
- He asks for the key to your storage room, the place where you protect your wealth and treasure, so that he can use what you have in ways that fulfill the vision of his Kingdom.
- He asks for the key to your kitchen and dining room so that he can guide the stewardship of your body and give you compassion for a hungry world.
- He asks for the key to your bedroom so that his love can permeate your human loves and passions and be present in the most intimate relationships of your life.
- He asks for the key to that private little closet, the one where you hide the things you don't want anyone else to see—the inner sanctum or mission control center—so that his will takes control of everything you think, say, or do.
- Imagine that as you relinquish control of your life you begin to experience the inexhaustible resources of the Spirit of God at work within your heart until you are filled with the fullness of God's love.

4
THE COMPANY OF THE COMMITTED

I was sitting around a retreat center table with some pastoral colleagues. All of us had experienced the exuberating joys and the devastating defeats of ministry in a local congregation. Our attention was focused on one brother who had recently watched his wife die with cancer.

We listened as he told us about how he, his children, and his congregation made that painful journey. He said that the single most difficult moment was when he took off his wedding ring. We sat together in a moment of stunned and sacred silence. Then one of us asked him, "What's been the most helpful thing for you along the way?"

Our friend paused. He looked each of us in the eye. Then he moved his hand around the circle with his palm open and his finger pointing to the friends around the table as he simply said, "This." He poked

> "Church is the primary place we have for learning this language of love…a gathering of people who are committed to learning the language in the company of the Trinity and in company with one another."[1]
> —Eugene Peterson

his best friend in the ribs and said, "This guy has always been there when I needed him."

In that moment, I knew I had seen what it means to be the church, the body of Christ, the community of brothers and sisters who bear one another's burdens and, by doing so, fulfill the law of Christ (Galatians 6:2).

The journey toward Christian perfection is always personal, but it is never private. We grow toward perfection in the company of other imperfect disciples. We learn the way to holiness in the community of faith. We work out our sanctification in the relationships, institutions, economic systems, and political structures of the world around us.

Benjamin Ingham marked a decisive moment in his search for the holy life when he wrote, "We appointed to meet every Friday night...to read and encourage one another."[2] This weekly meeting continued the entire time Ingham lived in Oxford.[3] Ingham discovered the power of Christian community in forming a life that is centering in loving God and loving others. I remember hearing E. Stanley Jones say that everyone who belongs to Christ belongs to everyone who belongs to Christ. We walk the way of holiness as one and as many.

One Out of Many

One of the less remembered actions of Congress on July 4, 1776, was to elect a committee to design a seal for the new United States of America. That committee submitted its proposal on August 20, but it wasn't approved. Six years and two committees later, Congress approved the Great Seal that appears on your passport, the front of the president's podium, and the back of the dollar bill. The design element goes all the way back to the initial proposal in 1776, with the eagle holding a ribbon in its beak with the words *E Pluribus Unum*, meaning "Out of many, one."[4]

Those words were the de facto motto of the United States until 1956, when Congress adopted "In God We Trust," but the original words are rich in meaning. "Out of many, one" lifts the vision of different people from diverse places, races, and cultures being drawn together into "one nation, indivisible, with liberty and justice for all."[5]

We've not yet perfected that vision. There have always been forces at work to make us "many out of one" instead of "one out of many." The venomous forces of nonnegotiable political ideologies keep pulling us apart with little or no regard for what the Pilgrim founders called "the common good." But even our money continues to affirm that *E Pluribus Unum* is the goal toward which we should be moving.

Paul confronted the "many-out-of-one" spirit in his letter to the Corinthians. It was the most contentious and conflicted congregation he planted. That's why he wrote:

There are different spiritual gifts but the same Spirit; and there are different ministries and the same Lord; and there are different activities but the same God who produces all of them in everyone. A demonstration of the Spirit is given to each person for the common good. (1 Corinthians 12:4-7)

He reprised the same theme in his letter to the Ephesians:

Conduct yourselves with all humility, gentleness, and patience. Accept each other with love, and make an effort to preserve the unity of the Spirit with the peace that ties you together. You are one body and one spirit, just as God also called you in one hope. There is one Lord, one faith, one baptism, and one God and Father of all, who is over all, through all, and in all.
(Ephesians 4:1-6)

Paul repeats the word *one* seven times to make the point that when the Holy Spirit is alive in and among the followers of Jesus Christ, the many become one in Christ.

E Pluribus Unum doesn't mean that we become bland computer copies of each other. Followers of Christ are not homogenized into spiritual sameness. In both letters, Paul celebrates the amazing diversity of the many who become one in Christ.

In the same way the Spirit brooded over chaos in the Book of Genesis and brought forth the infinite variety of creation, the Holy Spirit is at work in the lives of baptized followers of Jesus Christ to release an almost infinite variety of gifts, all of which, Paul says, are united in one common purpose: "to equip God's people for the work of serving and building up the body of Christ until we all reach the unity of faith and knowledge of God's Son" (Ephesians 4:12-13).

The *E Pluribus Unum* way of life runs directly against the grain of a culture that lives by what the *New York Times* accurately called "The Gospel According to Me." The writers said that many people in the Western democracies have traded the idea of a single, omnipotent deity for "a weak, but all-pervasive idea of spiritually tied to a personal ethic of authenticity and a liturgy of inwardness." As a result, "well-being has become the primary goal of human life."[6] You could call it the "selfie" culture that assumes the things that matter most are always within arm's reach.

43

In contrast, no one travels the road toward Christian perfection alone. The path of holiness draws us deeper into the lives of others so that using our gifts for the common good takes priority over our personal well-being. Often to our surprise, we discover along the way that our well-being is bound up in the well-being of others. But living with others in the body of Christ is never as easy as it sounds.

Who's In? Who's Out?

Who would be inside and who would be outside the Christian community was a persistent problem in the early church. On Pentecost, the Holy Spirit moved into the lives of all kinds of people who spoke all kinds of languages from all kinds of nations, races, and cultures (see Acts 2:1-12). Given that experience, you might think that the answer to the question "Who's in?" was indisputably clear: "*Everyone* who calls on the name of the Lord will be saved" (Acts 2:21, emphasis added). Case closed. Everybody who calls is in! But it wasn't that easy. It still isn't.

The early Christians wrestled with questions about God's law in the Old Testament:

- What about Gentiles who were outside the covenant with Abraham?
- What about an Ethiopian eunuch (Acts 8:26-39)? God's law specifically banned him.
- What about circumcision? God required it under the old covenant. Do we have to follow that law in the body of Christ?
- What about the kosher laws regarding food? God told us what to eat and what not to eat.
- Who's in? Who's out?

Faithful disciples in every generation have faced similar questions in one way or another. On one side are folks who see the church primarily as an exclusive gathering of those who are saved and living up to the highest standards of the gospel. On the other side are folks who see the church in Jesus' metaphor of the dragnet that picks up all kinds, gathering people wherever they are and calling them to follow Christ (see Matthew 13:47).

My conviction is that because our belief that God's grace is available to everyone, disciples in the Wesleyan tradition ought to fall on the dragnet side of that question. We believe that the grace of God meets us wherever we are—

just the way Jesus met the first disciples, including Peter, along the seashore—calling us to follow Christ in a lifelong journey of transformation. And this belief encompasses all.

The Second Conversion of Peter

Have you ever had a dream that was so real you could taste it? I think that's what happened to Peter when he went up on the roof one day at noon to pray. He was hungry, and while lunch was being prepared, he fell asleep. In Acts 10, we read that in his dream he saw the heavens opened—the way they opened for Jacob when he dreamed of a ladder connecting heaven and earth (see Genesis 28:10-22). Peter saw a large sheet being lowered in front of him, filled with "all kinds of four-legged animals, reptiles, and wild birds" (v. 12). The one thing they had in common is that, according to Old Testament law, they were all unclean. Peter recognized the voice of the Risen Christ saying, "Get up, Peter! Kill and eat!" (v. 13). Peter blurted out, "Absolutely not, Lord! I have never eaten anything impure or unclean" (v. 14).

It wasn't the first time Peter had said, "No way!" to his Lord. It takes us back to that last Passover meal when Jesus wanted to wash Peter's feet and his first response was, "You will never wash my feet!" (John 13:8).

The voice spoke again, "Never consider unclean what God has made pure" (v. 15). It happened three times, just as Peter had denied he knew Jesus three times (see John 18:15-27) and Jesus later gave Peter the opportunity to affirm his love for him three times (see John 21:15-19). You could say that Peter was a slow learner. You also could say that he was a lot like every one of us.

Luke records, "Peter was bewildered about the meaning of the vision" (v. 17), which has to be a major understatement of the internal conflict he was experiencing. God's law on the matter was

> "Everyone needs a group fellowship in which the group is in a conspiracy of love to make and keep each member the best person he is capable of being."[7]
> —E. Stanley Jones

perfectly clear (see Leviticus 11). Any faithful Jew would have died of starvation before eating any of the stuff in that sheet.

That's when three strangers knocked at Peter's gate. They had come from a Gentile named Cornelius, who was considered to be just as unclean as the animals in that sheet. Peter faced a gut-wrenching choice. Would he disobey

God's law by associating with Gentiles? Or would he obey God's Spirit by going with them to Cornelius's house? Still confused, Peter made an earth-shaking decision. "Peter invited them into the house as his guests. The next day he got up and went with them" (v. 23).

When they arrived at Cornelius's house, Cornelius fell at Peter's feet as a way of honoring him, but "Peter lifted him up, saying, 'Get up! Like you, I'm just a human'" (v. 26). This affirmation of their common humanity was no small thing for a faithful Jew who believed he was one of God's chosen people. Peter acknowledged this when he said to the crowd gathered around Cornelius's house: "You all realize that it is forbidden for a Jew to associate or visit with out-siders. However, God has shown me that I should never call a person impure or unclean" (v. 28). He made the point of the story perfectly clear in verses 34-36:

> *"I really am learning that God doesn't show partiality to one group of people over another. Rather, in every nation, whoever worships him and does what is right is acceptable to him. This is the message of peace he sent to the Israelites by proclaiming the good news through Jesus Christ: He is Lord of all!"*

Peter proclaimed the good news of what God had done in Jesus Christ. The Holy Spirit fell on the folks in Cornelius's house just as the Spirit had come upon the first apostles on Pentecost so that "the circumcised believers who had come with Peter were astonished that the gift of the Holy Spirit had been poured out even on the Gentiles" (v. 45).

Peter's relationship with Cornelius marked a significant revolution in both his life and his faith. Equally as dramatic as Paul's conversion on the Damascus Road, it was nothing less than a moment of conversion of Peter. It became a pivotal story for the early church because it didn't end there.

The church leaders in Jerusalem were shocked that Peter had been hanging out with Gentiles. But when they heard Peter's story, "they calmed down. They praised God and concluded, 'So then God has enabled Gentiles to change their hearts and lives so that they might have new life'" (Acts 11:18).

What do we do with a story like this? More important, what does this story do with us?

The spiritual crisis for Peter was not about whether or not he would eat unclean food. The issue was not in his digestive tract but in his heart. It was about whether he would be in relationship with people whom he had been conditioned to see as unclean, outside the boundary of God's grace.

Out of the struggle against apartheid in South Africa, Peter Storey wrote, "Just as the baby of a mother addicted to crack-cocaine is born a drug addict, human beings are born with *an addiction to division and exclusion*. We will if we can, always find a fashionable prejudice that puts us on the inside and as many people as possible on the outside."[8] This inbred tendency for division is tangible evidence of what theologians call "original sin."

We all stand in need of the kind of conversion that Peter experienced on the seashore and that Paul experienced on the way to Damascus—a conversion that awakens us to new life in Christ. But we also need the kind of conversion Peter experienced in his rooftop dream. If one is conversion to loving God, the other is conversion in the way we love others and are willing to accept into our lives and communities the people we have excluded.

Peter Storey said that it is never enough to simply pray, "Come into my heart, Lord Jesus." He wrote, "When we pray that prayer, Jesus responds, 'Can I bring my friends?'" He went on to describe our hard-hearted response: "We look at those clustered round him and say, 'O my God, not *them*...Lord, do you *really* want me to let them into my heart, too?'...And Jesus says, 'Love me, love my friends.'"[9]

If we believe that being made perfect in love means loving others the way they are loved by God (Matthew 5:43-48), then we need to be ready for the same kind of surprises that came to Peter when God taught him never to consider any other person as "unclean" (Acts 10:28). The challenge is to find the way to practice that kind of love in the context of our personal relationships and our local congregations.

Living with Our Differences

There is no one-size-fits-all pattern for the way local congregations demonstrate that they have learned the lesson Peter learned in his rooftop dream, but given the growing diversity in our world, every biblically-faithful congregation is called to find their unique way of demonstrating God's radically inclusive love.

One of the core values that continues to determine the ministry at Hyde Park United Methodist Church, where I served for twenty-two years, is that along with being Christ centered and biblically rooted, the church is open minded. The church often describes that value in terms of concentric circles. The nonnegotiable center of our life and ministry is defined by the gospel, the Apostles' Creed, our Methodist spiritual tradition, and the mission and core values of the congregation. Grounded in those central commitments, we are able to allow space for equally faithful disciples to come to different conclusions about how they apply the gospel to matters that are on the circumference of our life together. It's not a difference of importance but a difference of location.

Our experience was that the more intentionally we moved into the center, the more we were able to live together with varieties of conviction about the things that are on the circumference. The closer we came to one another, the more we were able to live with the differences that otherwise would have divided us. This way of being the church is not for folks who need rigid boundaries around every doctrine or decision, but it is a place for open-minded disciples whose primary commitment is to love God and love others.

John Wesley gave the classic expression to this way of living together in his sermon on "The Catholic Spirit" (he used the word *catholic* to mean "universal"):

> Though we cannot think alike, may we not love alike?
> May we not be of one heart, though we are not of one
> opinion? Without all doubt, we may. Herein all the
> children of God may unite, notwithstanding these smaller
> differences. These remaining as they are, they may
> forward one another in love and in good works....
>
> But while he is steadily fixed in his religious principles in
> what he believes to be the truth as it is in Jesus...his heart
> is enlarged toward all mankind, those he knows and those
> he does not; he embraces with strong and cordial affection
> neighbours and strangers, friends and enemies. This is
> catholic or universal love....For love alone gives the title
> to this character.[10]

The Wesley brothers' faith was molded in a time of divisive religious tension and political conflict in England. Paul Wesley Chilcote writes that Wesley "was always seeking third alternatives through which to articulate and live his faith over against the divisive polarities of his age."[11]

Living with and sometimes engaging in the tendentious debates within my own denomination, I have become convinced that Wesley's "Catholic Spirit" is an essential model for faithful disciples who are growing in love and grace. It also could be the transformational witness of the gospel in our deeply divided culture. The either/or dualism with which we tend to approach decision making is more consistent with the many-out-of-one attitude in Corinth than with the way of Jesus in the Gospels or the work of the Holy Spirit in the Book of Acts. The way of the Trinity is always *E Pluribus Unum*.

Our Way in the World

So, as a community of imperfect disciples on the way to perfection, how do we make our way in a world that often functions in ways that are a direct contradiction of our vision of the kingdom of God? How can the "company of the committed" become the source of strength for the way we live and serve?

Every two weeks the women of Phakamisa gather for training at the Pinetown Methodist Church near Durban, South Africa. The Zulu word *phakamisa* means "to lift up."[12] It's a ministry that trains women to be preschool teachers and child-care workers in the impoverished townships scattered around the city. Their day begins in worship and prayer. The pattern is powerful in its simplicity. The women sing an African gospel song or a traditional hymn set to a rhythmic beat. Their unaccompanied voices fill the room with sound. They then pause for silence until one of the women rises to share what has happened in her life since their last meeting. They pray for her concerns, sing again, listen once more, and pray again.

Because of the linguistic deficiency of the mission team from our congregation, they provided a woman to sit with each of us to translate what the women were saying. Veronica whispered into my ear in English what the women were saying in Zulu. Some of the stories were painful accounts of elementary-age children who were now the heads of their homes because their parents and grandparents had died of HIV-AIDS. Some were accounts of courage in the face of poverty, hunger, rape, and injustice. At one point Veronica hesitated before translating and said, "Ah, this is so terrible."

It was all rather overwhelming. Then the last woman got up. She wanted to read from the Book of Joshua. I pulled a Bible out of the pew rack and found the place to follow along with her:

> No one shall be able to stand against you all the days of your life. As I was with Moses, so I will be with you; I will not fail you or forsake you. Be strong and courageous; for you shall put this people in possession of the land that I swore to their ancestors to give them. Only be strong and very courageous, being careful

> *to act in accordance with all the law that my servant Moses commanded you; do not turn from it to the right hand or to the left, so that you may be successful wherever you go.... I hereby command you: Be strong and courageous; do not be frightened or dismayed, for the LORD your God is with you wherever you go." (Joshua 1:5-9 NRSV)*

After the reading, all of the women began to pray aloud at the same time. I could not understand a single word, but the sound of their voices felt like a gentle summer rain falling on the ground around us. It was as if all the pain they had shared was sanctified, made holy, as it was washed in the grace of God, renewing and strengthening them the way the rain renews the earth. I kept hearing those words that are repeated three times in the text, "Be strong and courageous," and the final promise: "do not be frightened or dismayed, for the LORD your God is with you wherever you go" (v. 9).

When the voices became silent, the women stood up. One woman took the Christ candle from the altar and started down the aisle. Row by row they processed out of the sanctuary and back into the challenges of the impoverished world they serve, singing along the way, "We are walking in the light of God."

All I could say was, "That's the Spirit!" That's the Spirit of God alive in the very real struggles of our life together as the body of Christ. That's what it means for the Holy Spirit to come as the Advocate, Counselor, and strong Comforter who leads us into the world as the agents of God's love and grace.

That's the way the Spirit can come to us too. The same Spirit who spoke the words, "Be strong and courageous" to the women of Phakamisa is the Spirit who sustains us as imperfect disciples in an imperfect world on the way to perfection. In the "company of the committed," we find strength in the promise, "The LORD your God is with you wherever you go." (v. 9).

5
ON FIRE WITH HOLY LOVE

George Foster was a feisty Florida preacher with the stature of a Hobbit and the energy of a cage boxer. I've never forgotten the energy with which he once quoted John Wesley's words to George Shadford: "I let you lose, George, on the great continent of America. Publish your message in the open face of the sun, and do all the good you can."[1]

The passion with which George Foster shared Wesley's challenge made me want more of the kind of fire in the bones (Jeremiah 20:9) that he had. He demonstrated what Paul was talking about when he told the disciples in Rome to "be on fire in the Spirit as you serve the Lord!" (Romans 12:11).

Charles Wesley described this spiritual fire in a hymn:

> O Thou who camest from above,
> The pure *celestial* fire to impart,
> Kindle a *flame of sacred love*
> Upon the mean altar of my heart.
>
> There let it for thy glory *burn*
> With *inextinguishable blaze*,
> And trembling to its source return,
> In humble prayer and fervent praise.
>
> Jesus, confirm my heart's desire
> To work and speak and think for thee;
> Still let me guard the *holy fire*,
> And still stir up thy gift in me.[2]
> (emphasis added)

The words *celestial fire, flame of sacred love, burn, inextinguishable blaze,* and *holy fire* capture the heart of the Wesleyan revival that began when John Wesley felt his heart "strangely warmed." Wesley and his followers lived and served with an undeniable passion, evidenced by:

- the heartfelt urgency with which the early Methodists preached,
- the relentless energy with which Francis Asbury and the Methodist "circuit riders" crisscrossed the American colonies,
- the enthusiasm with which Methodism spread around the globe,
- and the conviction with which Methodist people through the years have fed the hungry; confronted injustice; tackled poverty; and labored for the rights of women, children, and minorities.

"My God ... may this holy flame ever warm my breast, that I may serve you with all my might; and let it consume in my heart all selfish desires, that I may in all things regard not myself but you."[3] —John Wesley

When we disciples in the Methodist tradition have been at our best, we have been a people whose hearts are on fire with a passionate desire to share God's love and to participate in God's transformation of the kingdoms of this world into the kingdom of God.

A Place for Passion

Sam Keen has said that the most common variety of stress is "rustout" rather than "burnout." He wrote, "It is a product, not of an excess of fire but of a deficiency of passion."[4] I would argue that we could say that same thing about many of our congregations today.

- It's not a lack of good intentions or of honorable attempts to do good things, but a "deficiency of passion" for taking on the deeper challenges of forming disciples who become a part of God's transformation of the world.
- It's not that we do not affirm the creeds but that we are not energetically engaged in the costly journey toward Christian perfection.

- It's not that we do not believe in God but that we seldom expect the God in whom we believe to actually do something in and through our lives that makes a transformative difference in us and in the world.
- It's not that we don't care enough but that we are not joyful enough to actually convince the world that the gospel might be what all of us are most deeply searching for.
- It's not that we are bad but that we are far too boring.

The one thing that we disciples may need to be more effective witnesses in this world is heartfelt passion—the fire of divine love.

A Passionate God

The billboard would have been hard to miss. It was strategically placed along a busy section of the Interstate. The white words popped out against a solid black background announcing, "God is not angry" with a website beneath it. My first thought was, "Really?"

On one hand, I appreciated a creative attempt to counter the negative images of God that tend to permeate a biblically illiterate culture with a surprising witness to God's love and grace. The billboard was not cheap. Whoever put it there really wanted to reach people for Christ by letting them know that God was not angry with them. There was something downright Wesleyan about the evangelistic passion behind it. It reminded me of the way John Wesley said he "submitted to be more vile and proclaimed in the highways the glad tidings of salvation."[5] But my second response led me to ask some hard questions:

- Is God the passionless "unmoved mover" who looks on the world from a distance but is never engaged in or enraged by what goes on in it?
- Does saying that God is not angry suggest that the Old Testament reveals a God of wrath while the New Testament reveals a God of love? (This kind of response to the Old Testament was rejected by the church in A.D. 140.)
- Aren't there things in this world about which we want God to be angry?
- Haven't they read the Bible? According to Scripture, God does experience anger along with a lot of other emotions.

The God revealed to us in Scripture loves this world so deeply and cares about it so passionately that God:

- laughs at our human arrogance (Psalm 2:2-4),
- rejoices over us (Zephaniah 3:17),
- weeps with us beside the grave (John 11:33-35),
- cries over our inability to make peace (Luke 19:41),
- is angered by our acts of injustice (Luke 19:45-46),
- and is brokenhearted by the way his people reject his love (Hosea 11:8).

The writer of the letter to the Hebrews pointed toward the passionate heart of God by saying that "our God really is a consuming fire" (Hebrews 12:29). He was reclaiming the words from the Book of Deuteronomy:

> *So all of you, watch yourselves! Don't forget the covenant that the LORD your God made with you by making an idol or an image of any kind or anything the LORD your God forbids, because the LORD your God is an all-consuming fire. He is a passionate God.*
> *(Deuteronomy 4:23-24)*

I take it as good news to know that God is not a passive or unresponsive observer of the injustice, suffering, and pain of a sin-infected, violence-addicted world. God cares passionately about this world. God hurts with the hungry. God is angry when children are abused or neglected. God is passionate about injustice. God is brokenhearted by our rebellion and sin.

To believe in the Incarnation—that God became flesh in Jesus Christ—is to know that the infinite God has entered into the finite hurts and hopes, weakness and strength, light and the darkness, joy and sorrow, sin and death that are a part of our lives in this broken and imperfect creation. That's why the writer could say, "We don't have a priest who is out of touch with our reality. He's been through weakness and testing, experienced it all—all but the sin" (Hebrews 4:15, *The Message*).

The questions become:

- How does belief in a passionate God transform the way we live?
- If our God is really a consuming fire, what will it look like for that fire to burn through us?

A Passion for the Personal

There is a deeply personal answer to those questions. The way to holiness always takes us through "the refiner's fire" (Malachi 3:2). The journey of Christian perfection always includes the way the Holy Spirit purifies our intentions and burns away anything that prevents us from becoming all that God intends for us to be. The fire of God's presence sets our hearts aflame with a burning desire for our lives to be a part of God's work of healing and transformation in the world. The fire of God's love ignites a personal passion within us to share that love with people who have not yet experienced it.

My father was the kind of Methodist who had that fire in his bones. He was only fifty-nine years old when he lost his battle with cancer and was raised to the new life of the resurrection. He was a Depression-era child from what we would consider today to be a poor family, living on a little farm where my grandparents somehow raised six children in a four-room house. Their first-born had died as an infant in the flu pandemic of 1918.

My father dreamed of going to college, but instead he and his three brothers went off to World War II. I'm named for the brother who didn't return. Like the rest of "the greatest generation," he came back and went to work, raising a family and building an auto parts business out of nothing. The summer before I went to college, the business burned down and he had to rebuild it.

He was a simple man whose life was grounded in a few unshakable commitments to his family, his business, and his faith. There were times when we questioned whether the business took priority over the family, but there was no question about the priority he placed on his faith. Everyone who knew him knew that he was a Christian, a Methodist, and a teetotaler—in that order.

He would open the store to get a part for the mechanic at a local service station on Sunday, but only after he had been to Sunday school and worship. He was the guy people would call on to give a prayer before dinner because they knew that he knew how to pray. He never hesitated to share his faith by serving as a lay speaker or a representative of the Methodist Men.

When he died, we heard the untold stories from people he had helped when they were down and out across the years. He ensured that his witness would continue beyond his death through the words that are carved in his gravestone: "I commend my Savior to you." He had learned that those words are carved on a statue of Charles Wesley in Bristol, England, and he claimed them as his own.

Throughout his life, he lived with a heartwarming passion for others to become disciples of Jesus Christ.

To be a disciple in the Wesleyan tradition is to experience a deeply personal, heart-burning passion to share the love of God we have experienced in Christ with men and women who have not yet experienced it. That same heart-warming fire sends us into the world as the agents of that love.

More Than a Warm Heart

Peter Storey pointed out that being Methodist is "more than a warmed heart—but never less."[6] In the Wesleyan tradition, discipleship that begins in the individual heart is lived out in community with others. Holiness that is nurtured in "works of piety" becomes a tangible reality through "works of mercy." The same fire of love that warms the heart ignites a passion within us to demonstrate that love in active service and social justice.

In one of his sermons on Jesus' Sermon on the Mount, John Wesley declared, "Christianity is essentially a social religion; and that to turn it into a solitary religion, is indeed to destroy it."[7] He responded to the questions that came from people who tried to contain the Christian life within the confines of personal spirituality—questions that have a distinctly contemporary ring—with these words:

> What need of loading it with *doing* and *suffering*? . . . Is it
> not enough . . . to soar upon the wings of love? Will it not
> suffice to worship God . . . without encumbering ourselves
> with outward things, or even thinking of them at all? Is
> it not better, that the whole extent of our thought should
> be taken up with high and heavenly contemplation; and
> that instead of busying ourselves at all about externals, we
> should only commune with God in our hearts?[8]

Wesley called the desire for this kind of individually internalized spirituality a "pleasing delusion."[9] It is the continuing delusion of everyone who attempts to limit the Christian life to personal piety. While Wesley affirmed that the root of the Christian life is in the heart, he was convinced that the root must, of necessity, extend its branches into the world. At the same time, he declared in the eighteenth-century vernacular that "bare outside religion which has no root in the heart, is nothing worth."[10] Borrowing language from the marriage liturgy, he said, "God hath joined them together from the beginning of the world; and let not man put them asunder."[11]

Peter Storey affirmed Wesley's words when he said that "there is no 'personal' Gospel, no 'social' Gospel: There is only the *whole* gospel, expressed both personally and socially."[12]

Being made perfect in love includes the process by which the Holy Spirit empowers us to be the agents of God's love and grace in the world. The goal is both a warm heart and a transformed world. Discipleship in the Wesleyan tradition always combines the inner life of personal piety with the outward witness of evangelistic passion and social action. This includes the way we live out the gospel in the often-conflicted arena of our political life.

On Mixing Religion and Politics

Those who think that religion and politics should never mix should take a good look at history. For good or ill, what we believe in our hearts gets worked out in human society through the social, political, and economic systems in which we live.

The fact is that religion and politics have always been, and always will be, mixed up together in this world. Like any good recipe, the trick is in getting the mix right. Confuse a "dash of salt" with a "dish of salt," and you'll end up with some really bad fudge. Without salt, Jesus said, things become tasteless. But being the "salt of the earth" as he described (Matthew 5:13) doesn't mean turning everything around us into blocks of salt or losing our saltiness in the baking.

Mix in too much religion or the wrong kind of theology, and politics become lethal. It was, after all, Bible-based, religion-soaked politics that birthed the Crusades, led to the Spanish Inquisition, burned New England witches at the stake, supported slavery in the American South, fed the fires of the Holocaust, and laid the foundation for apartheid in South Africa.

Mix in too much political power, and religion loses its integrity and becomes the servant of the state. Whenever Christianity is merged with political and economic power, the prophetic witness of Scripture and Jesus' vision of the kingdom of God is weakened or lost in the mix. To change the metaphor, the marriage of the church, which the New Testament calls the Bride of Christ, with any national agenda, economic system, or political party results in the church becoming an abused spouse.

But when Christians get the mix right, good things can happen. It was the fire of Christian passion that inspired William Wilberforce to work for the abolition of slavery in the British Empire; that led to child labor reform in the United States; that inspired Martin Luther King, Jr. in the movement for civil rights; that sustained Desmond Tutu in the struggle against apartheid; and that continues to hold up the vision of peace and social justice in our world today.

Evangelical theologian and activist Shane Claiborne gets the mix right when he says that the question is not whether Christians are political, but *how* they are political. He said, "We need to be politically engaged, but peculiar in how we engage.... To be nonpartisan doesn't mean we're nonpolitical. We should refuse to get sucked into political camps and insist on pulling the best out of all of them."[13]

The continuing challenge for faithful disciples is to live in faithful obedience to Christ while being responsible citizens of the community and nation of which we are a part.

Where Religion and Politics Mix

The story of Jesus' journey to the cross points to a time when the religious and political power players of the day found common ground in their rejection of Jesus.

In Luke's Gospel, the Passion story begins with the religious leaders "looking for a way to kill Jesus" (Luke 22:2). After the mockery of justice in Jesus' trial before Pilate and his appearance before Herod, Luke records, "Pilate and Herod became friends with each other that day. Before this, they had been enemies" (Luke 23:12). There's nothing like a common enemy to make strange bedfellows. The cross was the place where religion and politics became united in their determination to get rid of the One whose words and way undermined their power.

One of the places where religion and politics got the mixture right was in the witness of Martin Luther King, Jr. It is impossible to read his sermons and miss the way he was rooted in a biblical vision of freedom and justice and found ways to use the political system to bring fundamental change in the American culture. To remember Dr. King solely as a political leader is to miss the prophetic "fire in the bones" he demonstrated when he spoke to our nation in the spirit of Jeremiah, Isaiah, Amos, and Jesus.

The challenge for imperfect disciples living in an imperfect political and economic system is to allow the biblical vision to define our politics without allowing our politics to define the biblical vision.

Now and then someone will ask me, "Are you conservative or liberal?" The way they ask the question always conveys which answer they will accept. My answer, which I also pray to be my consistent commitment, is that I'm not concerned about liberal or conservative. I just want to be faithful. Sometimes that means conservatives think I'm liberal, and sometimes it means that liberals

> "God's way of doing justice in this deeply disordered world is always imperfect, because he does it through deeply flawed people.... But in the actions of otherwise imperfect people we see God at work through his human instruments."[14]
> —Fleming Rutledge

think I'm conservative. My guess is that if I keep both groups unhappy, I may be close to getting it right. The only thing that matters is whether I am acting in ways that are consistent with Jesus' vision of the kingdom of God.

Readers of *Rolling Stone* magazine were surprised when Pope Francis appeared on the cover of the magazine. Here's what the lead editorial said:

> His recognizable humanity comes off as positively
> revolutionary.... By eschewing the papal palace for a
> modest two-room apartment, by publicly scolding church
> leaders for being "obsessed" with divisive social issues...
> by devoting much of his first major written teaching to a
> scathing critique of unchecked free-market capitalism, the
> pope revealed his own obsessions to be more in line with
> the boss' son.[15]

An obsession "to be more in line with the boss' son" should be the raging fire within the heart of every disciple of Jesus Christ. This obsession to become more and more like Jesus is the source of our passion, the light for our path, the refining fire that purifies our intentions, and the energizing force that sustains our discipleship over the long haul of Christian perfection.

6
ALL THE WAY TO HEAVEN

> We're marching to Zion,
> Beautiful, beautiful Zion;
> We're marching upward to Zion,
> The beautiful city of God.[1]

The hymn "Marching to Zion," is a bold affirmation that our discipleship is always going somewhere, always moving upward, always pointed in the direction of the fullness of God's salvation for our lives and this creation. It's another way of saying that Christian perfection is "an end without an ending." It is the end or goal toward which God's saving work is always moving. Followers of Christ are always marching upward to Zion. The transformation that begins in our hearts ultimately will be fulfilled in heaven.

The biblical metaphor in the hymn is of pilgrims making their way to worship in the Temple on Mount Zion in Jerusalem. Psalms 120–134 traditionally are considered to be the songs they sang along the way. Each psalm begins with the Hebrew ascription *Shir HaMa'alot*, which is translated, "A Song of Ascent."[2] E. Stanley Jones used that phrase as the title of his spiritual autobiography. He called it "my song of the pilgrimage I am making from what I was to what God is making of me...a Christian-in-the-making. Not yet 'made,' but only in the making at eighty-three."[3]

The New Testament writer of Hebrews drew on that pilgrim tradition to set our sights on the destination of our discipleship. Don't miss the way the descriptive phrases bubble out of the writer's imagination, each one building in intensity until they culminate in the presence of Jesus:

61

> *But you have drawn near to Mount Zion, the city of the living God, heavenly Jerusalem, to countless angels in a festival gathering, to the assembly of God's firstborn children who are registered in heaven, to God the judge of all, to the spirits of the righteous who have been made perfect, to Jesus the mediator of the new covenant." (Hebrews 12:22-24)*

Heaven is our destination. Mount Zion is always out ahead of us. Along the way of Christian perfection, the way ahead is always *forward*. God always has more for us in the future than we have had in the past. Perhaps this is why windshields are always larger than rearview mirrors.

Paul described his journey in a deeply autobiographical passage from his letter to the Philippians:

> *I do not consider myself to have "arrived", spiritually, nor do I consider myself already perfect. But I keep going on, grasping ever more firmly that purpose for which Christ grasped me.... I do concentrate on this: I leave the past behind and with hands outstretched to whatever lies ahead I go straight for the goal— my reward the honour of being called by God in Christ.*
> *(Philippians 3:13-14, J.B.P.)*

"I believe that heaven is a place of growth, the finite forever approaching the infinite but never becoming that infinite....To commune with God and to grow forever in his likeness— yes, but never to arrive—is a possible and perfect fulfillment of my being as a finite person."[5]
—E. Stanley Jones

Poet Robert Browning wrote in the spirit of the Apostle Paul when he said, "Ah, but a man's reach should exceed his grasp, / Or what's a heaven for?"[4]

One of the foundational assumptions of *A Disciple's Heart* is that salvation is not a one-time event but an ongoing process of heart transformation that begins before we make our first commitment to Christ and continues throughout our life journey—all the way to heaven. The New Testament images of heaven in the Book of Revelation are not given to provide information but orientation. They are imaginative visions by which we set the direction for our lives— the goal toward which we are moving.

Our vision of what life is like in heaven determines the way we live right now. Because followers of Christ have caught a vision of the way things will be when God's kingdom comes and God's will is done on earth as it is in heaven, we are driven by a divine dissatisfaction with the way things are. Our reach always exceeds our grasp—that's what heaven is for.

Marching Through the Valley

The journey to Zion is always upward, but it is not always easy. Yet even when the way of holiness is difficult, it is always good.

After completing his studies at Oxford, Benjamin Ingham returned to the village of Ossett in rural Yorkshire where he served as a preacher and teacher, starting a charity school to serve the poor children of the community. In his first letter to Wesley, he acknowledged the challenges of maintaining his spiritual discipline away from the supportive community in Oxford, saying, "Tis scarce possible to imagine how wicked the world is."[6]

In Chapter 12 of the Book of Hebrews, the writer reminds us of the endurance of those who have made this pilgrimage before us so that we won't become discouraged and give up along the way (vv. 1-3). The writer compares God to a loving parent who disciplines his children "for our benefit so that we can share his holiness" (v. 10). The letter acknowledges what we all know: "No discipline is fun while it lasts, but it seems painful at the time. Later, however, it yields the peaceful fruit of righteousness for those who have been trained by it" (v. 11).

Read through the Songs of Ascent (Psalm 120–134) and you will discover that they are not simplistic, cheerful ditties that deny how difficult the journey can be. They are, in fact, ruthlessly honest about the dark, painful, frightening places through which the pilgrim travels on the way to Mount Zion. The singing begins in a low place:

I cried out to the Lord when I was in trouble...

Oh, I'm doomed
  because I have been an immigrant in Meshech,
  because I've made my home among Kedar's tents.

I've lived far too long
  with people who hate peace. (Psalm 120:1, 5-6)

All we need to know about Meshech and Kedar is that they are about as far removed from where the psalmist wants to be as he can get. It's a long way to Mount Zion. Then, in Psalm 121, the pilgrim looks toward the mountains, asking the disturbing question, "Where will my help come from?" The answer comes back:

> *My help comes from the LORD …*
>
> *The LORD will protect you on your journeys—*
>   *whether going or coming—*
> *from now until forever from now. (Psalm 121:2, 8)*

In Psalm 123, the guilt-ridden pilgrim cries out, "Have mercy / because we've had more than enough shame" (v. 3). Psalm 124 describes the way the pilgrims would have drowned in raging waters if God had not been with them. Psalm 130 pleads for God's forgiveness. Psalm 132 contains the reminder of "all the ways [David] suffered" (v. 1).

The psalmists never promise that the pilgrimage will be continual happiness and peace. In fact, the pathway to Zion leads through:

- desert places where we experience an unquenched thirst for more of God's grace;
- soul-searching places where we ask hard questions about who God is and who we are;
- lonely places were we feel rejection and walk the pathway by ourselves;
- dark places where the light of God's Spirit reveals things that we hide in the inner closets of our hearts;
- tear-soaked places where we experience the full weight of loss, suffering, and death;
- heartbreaking places where we enter into the needs of others;
- angry places where we confront the injustice of a sin-broken world;
- burning places where the refining fire of the Spirit purifies our intentions;
- frightening places where we cannot see the next step we should take;
- cross-shaped places where we are called to die to old ways of living in order to experience the new life of resurrection.

We sing the Songs of Ascent not because they provide an escape from those dark places, but because they remind us of where we are going and of the One who walks with us. Even when the pathway leads us down through the valley, it is ultimately moving upward. Even in our loneliness we are never alone.

There is a disturbing consistency in the way the great saints of the faith describe the hard, painful places of their journey as the places where they experienced the most profound spiritual growth. The dark night of the soul, as Saint John of the Cross referred to it, is almost always the place where they experience the light of God's grace in ways they never knew before.

Early in my years of ministry, I learned an important lesson from a pastoral mentor. Speaking about one of our highly gifted, outwardly successful, overconfident colleagues, he said, "That guy would be a better pastor if he had suffered a little more." Looking back across my own pilgrimage, I know that I am a deeper, richer, more fully committed disciple because of some of the dark valleys through which I have walked. I know that I am a more patient, grace-filled pastor because of the times when I have been knocked off my high horse and brought to a place of humble acceptance of my defeats and failures. I'm grateful for the way God has been with me in the dark, difficult places along the way to Zion. But I'm also grateful that God didn't leave me in those places.

Even in the dark places, the Songs of Ascent reverberate with a joyful awareness of the presence of God. Psalm 121 claims the promise that God "won't fall asleep on the job" (Psalm 121:3). Psalm 122 lifts the vision of a place where God's justice reigns (see v. 5). Psalm 125 promises that the Lord "surrounds his people" even as the mountains surround Jerusalem (v. 2). Psalm 126 reminds the weary pilgrim of a time when "our mouths were suddenly filled with laughter; / our tongues were filled with joyful shouts" (v. 2). Psalm 132 dares to believe that God's promise to David won't be taken back (see v. 11). The final song brings us with joy to our destination where we gather in worship:

> Let us for this faith contend,
> Sure salvation is its end;
> Heaven already is begun,
> Everlasting life is won.[7]
> —Charles Wesley

> *All you who serve the LORD: bless the LORD right now!*
> *All you who minister in the LORD's house at night: bless God!*
> *Lift up your hands to the sanctuary*
> *and bless the LORD! (Psalm 134:1-2)*

The destination of our discipleship is never in doubt. We are marching to Zion, to the place where we, with Charles Wesley, are "lost in wonder, love, and praise."[8] Knowing where we are going begins to shape the way we live along the way.

"Why?" or "Why Not?"

As disciples who are on the way to heaven, we also experience a divine dissatisfaction with the world the way that it is—with all its violence, bigotry, racism, poverty, pain, and death. Our hearts are on fire with a passion for this world to become all that God intends for it to be. We live in the present in ways that are consistent with what we believe about the future. On the way to Mount Zion, we bear witness to how life will be when we arrive there.

I believe Edward Kennedy delivered one of the most eloquent eulogies of my lifetime at the funeral service for his assassinated brother Robert. He concluded his eulogy with these memorable words:

> My brother need not be idealized, or enlarged in death
> beyond what he was in life, to be remembered simply as a
> good and decent man, who saw wrong and tried to right
> it, saw suffering and tried to heal it, saw war and tried to
> stop it....
>
> As he said many times, in many parts of this nation, to
> those he touched and who sought to touch him: "Some
> men see things as they are and say why. I dream things
> that never were and say why not."[9]

As Christian disciples on our way to Zion, we are never satisfied with seeing this world the way it is and asking, "Why?" We are always seeing the way God intends for this world to be and asking, "Why not?" Why not be a part of God's kingdom coming on earth? Why not invest in making our lives and our world a little bit more like heaven?

There is, of course, a sad reality concerning the journey to Mount Zion. Not everyone who begins the pilgrimage makes it all the way to the end. Some give up along the way.

In his letters to the Colossians and to Philemon, Paul listed Demas as one of his missionary companions (see Colossians 4:14 and Philemon 1:24). But later, while he is a prisoner in Rome, there is a plaintive tone to the way Paul tells Timothy, "Demas has fallen in love with the present world and has deserted me" (2 Timothy 4:10). We never hear of Demas again.

Any of us, anywhere along the way, can decide that we've gone far enough. Any of us can decide that the demands are too difficult, the work too hard, the effort too intense. We can always stop somewhere along the journey of discipleship. We can stop growing and settle down along the way. The purpose of the letter to the Hebrews is to encourage faithful disciples not to give up but to keep moving toward their destination.

> *So strengthen your drooping hands and weak knees! Make straight paths for your feet so that if any part is lame, it will be healed rather than injured more seriously. Pursue the goal of peace along with everyone—and holiness as well, because no one will see the Lord without it. (Hebrews 12:12-14)*

By the grace of God and the power of the Holy Spirit, we can keep reaching out to what lies ahead for the sake of our high calling in Christ Jesus—all the way to heaven.

When I made my last trip to Pennsylvania to visit with my father before his death, I took along the master plan for the construction of the first building for St. Luke's Church in Orlando. After I had walked him through the plans, he looked up and said, "I'd sure like to be around long enough to see this completed." He paused and then went on to say, "But I guess that's how it always is. There's always something more you'd like to live a little bit longer to see." There always is. Our reach should always exceed our grasp. That's what heaven is for.

Growing and Singing All the Way

The way of holiness is the way of continuous growth in our relationship with God all the way to heaven. Just as E. Stanley Jones described himself as a "Christian-in-the-making" at age eighty-three, Elizabeth was one of those faithful people who never stopped growing. Some people called her "Ibs," but her grandchildren called her "Gager." It was the name by which her strength, laughter, wisdom, and faith were passed on as a beautiful gift, not only to her children, grandchildren, and great-grandchildren but also to the wide circle of their friends. She drew all of us into her life as if we had been born there.

I will never forget standing with her, her daughter-in-law, and her young grandsons beside the hospital bed where we said good-bye to her thirty-nine-year-old son before they turned off the machines and let him go. Gager and I took the sons outside and sat down beneath the arching branches of an ancient oak tree. With an inner strength that left me standing in amazement, she laid aside her own grief and focused all of her energy on the boys who would face life without the father they adored, the son she loved, and the friend for whom I will always give thanks.

Gager died at ninety-four after a long, difficult decline that robbed her, and all of us, of the beauty and vitality of her life. Her last gift to me came by surprise. In her desk they found a copy of something I had written years ago for the church newsletter. It was my own personal reflection on Psalm 1. A handwritten note said she wanted it to be included in her memorial service. It became a witness of her journey as well as mine:

> O life-giving God,
>> whose power surges through the whole creation,
> I want to grow like a tree.
> Not like a weed, Lord, or an overnight kudzu vine,
>> but like a strong, healthy tree,
>> patient enough to grow slowly,
>> but always growing,
>> always sinking deeper roots,
>> always stretching wider branches,
>> always reaching higher into the sky.
> Like a tree, Lord,
>> with roots deep enough to keep it strong
>> when a hurricane blows in from the Gulf.
> One day, Lord, the tree will fall.
>> It will have been here long enough.
>> Even sequoias die.
>> That's okay, Lord.
>> No tree lasts forever.
> But may my tree fall because it has lived its life fully,
>> richly, deeply, drawing everything it could from the soil
>> and giving back life to the rest of creation.

> May the fruit of my tree
> > be a gift of life to others.
> Thank you, Lord, for the soil in which you have planted me.
> > This is where I want to grow.
> > Like a tree beside the waters.
> > I want to grow.

One Methodist scholar pointed out that while all of Wesley's hymns begin on earth, they always end up in heaven. Just as faithful pilgrims sang the Songs of Ascent along the way to Mount Zion, we sing our song of faith as we continue to grow all the way through life into the new life of the resurrection.

It was Easter Sunday morning. We were singing the final hymn during which anyone who wants to sing the "Hallelujah" chorus is invited to come to the chancel, pick up a score, and join the choir. Halfway back in the congregation, my nine-year-old granddaughter tugged on my wife's arm and said,

> When I have lived to thee alone,
> Pronounce the welcome word,
> "Well done!"
> And let me take my place above;
> Enter into my Master's joy,
> And all eternity employ
> In praise, and ecstasy, and love.[10]
> —Charles Wesley

"Gamma, look at Gampa's face!" Then she made a shocked expression to mirror the look she saw on mine.

The shocked look on my face was an involuntary response when I saw my ninety-one-year-old mother step out of the pew and start down the aisle, leaning on her cane every step of the way. It expressed my concern about how she would make it down the aisle and up the steps into the chancel. Fortunately, my son-in-law got his arm around her and supported her all the way.

I grew up hearing my mother singing hymns at bedtime and in the kitchen; singing solos for weddings, funerals, and church revivals; and singing in the choir every Sunday morning. It was no surprise to me that she loves Handel's arrangement of the Book of Revelation's hymn of praise to the risen Christ. She probably knows it by heart. She asked the organist to play it as we processed out of the sanctuary at my father's funeral.

Mom doesn't sing much anymore. Time and asthma inhalers have taken a toll on her voice. But this was Easter Sunday morning, and she was determined to get in on the singing. After the service, she said she hoped I wasn't embarrassed. I told her I wasn't embarrassed, just concerned. She said, "Well, I don't know if I'll get to sing it again, so I wanted to sing it today."

She will, of course, sing it again someday, in fuller voice and renewed strength when she joins the heavenly choirs. That is the promise of Easter and the destination of our discipleship. But Mom got it right. You shouldn't pass up the opportunity to sing "Hallelujah" when you can, particularly when your great-grandchildren are watching. We sing our Song of Ascent all the way to heaven.

We end this study with the invitation to a journey toward Christian perfection that will be fulfilled in heaven. Along the way we join Wesleyan disciples in singing our Wesleyan Song of Ascent:

> Finish, then, thy new creation;
> Pure and spotless let us be.
> Let us see thy great salvation
> Perfectly restored in thee;
> Changed from glory into glory,
> Till in heaven we take our place,
> Till we cast our crowns before thee,
> Lost in wonder, love, and praise.[11]
> —Charles Wesley

Notes

Introduction

1. *King Lear*, Act 3, Scene 6, http://shakespeare.mit.edu/lear/lear.3.6.html.

2. Ella Fitzgerald, "Hard Hearted Hannah," http://www.metrolyrics.com/hard-hearted-hannah-lyrics-ella-fitzgerald.html.

3. John Wesley, "The Way to the Kingdom," http://www.umcmission.org/Find-Resources/John-Wesley-Sermons/Sermon-7-The-Way-to-the-Kingdom#sthash.krKEoqvk.dpuf.

4. Richard Heitzenrater, *Diary of an Oxford Methodist: Benjamin Ingham, 1733—1734* (Durham, NC: Duke University Press, 1985), 34–45.

5. "An Earnest Appeal to Men of Reason and Religion," *The Works of John Wesley*, ed. Thomas Jackson, 14 vols., 3rd ed. (London: Wesley Methodist Book Room, 1872; reprinted ed.: Grand Rapids: Zondervan, 1958–1959), Vol. VIII, 3–4.

6. "Thoughts Upon Methodism," *The Works of John Wesley*, ed. Thomas Jackson, XIII: 258.

7. "O for a Heart to Praise My God," Charles Wesley, *The United Methodist Hymnal* (Nashville: The United Methodist Publishing House, 1989), 417.

8. John Wesley, "The Almost Christian," http://www.umcmission.org/Find-Resources/John-Wesley-Sermons/Sermon-2-The-Almost-Christian.

Chapter 1

1. Cardinal John Newman, *An Essay on the Development of Christian Doctrine*, chap. 1, sec. 1, part 7, http://www.newmanreader.org/Works/development/chapter1.html.

2. Richard Heitzenrater, *Diary of an Oxford Methodist*, 1–2.

3. Howard and Margaret Brown, "Follow, I Will Follow Thee," copyright 1935, renewed 1962.

4. Albert Schweitzer, *The Quest of the Historical Jesus* (New York: Macmillan, 1964), 403, http://www.earlychristianwritings.com/schweitzer/chapter20 .html.

5. John Wesley, "Advice to a People Called Methodists," http://www. umcmission.org/Find-Resources/John-Wesley-Sermons/The-Wesleys-and -Their-Times/Advice-to-a-People-Called-Methodist.

6. *The Book of Discipline of the United Methodist Church*—2012. Copyright © 2012 by The United Methodist Publishing House; ¶330, p. 250, http://issuu .com/abingdonpress/docs/9781426718120_online_part1/265.

7. Kathleen Norris, *Amazing Grace: A Vocabulary of Faith* (New York: Riverhead Books, 1998), 55.

8. Ibid, 56.

9. Heitzenrater, *Diary of an Oxford Methodist*, 31–32.

10. Paul Wesley Chilcote, *John & Charles Wesley: Selections from Their Writing and Hymns,* (Woodstock, VT: Skylight Paths, 2011), 144.

11. Thomas Merton, *Life and Holiness* (New York: Herder and Herder, 1963), 7.

12. "A Plain Account of Christian Perfection," *The Works of John Wesley,* ed. Thomas Jackson, XI: 367–368.

13. Eugene Peterson, *Practice Resurrection* (Grand Rapids: Eerdmans, 2010), 6.

14. Magrey R. deVega, "Monumental Moments," in *The Midweek Message*, St. Paul's United Methodist Church, Cherokee, Iowa, September 4, 2012, http://mdevega.blogspot.com/2012/09/monumental-moments.html.

15. "What Is Our Calling's Glorious Hope," Charles Wesley, 1742, http://www .hymnary.org/text/what_is_our_callings_glorious_hope.

16. deVega, "Monumental Moments."

Chapter 2

1. Heitzenrater, *Diary of an Oxford Methodist*, 109.

2. James Tozer, "Is it a sin? Christian words deleted from Oxford dictionary," *The Daily Mail*, December 7, 2008, http://www.dailymail.co.uk/news /article-1092668/Is-sin-Christian-words-deleted-Oxford-dictionary .html#ixzz3E8vggsmW.

3. Karl Menninger, *Whatever Became of Sin?* (New York: Hawthorne Books, 1973), 17.

4. Ibid., 19.

5. William Willimon, *Who Will Be Saved?* (Nashville: Abingdon Press, 2008), 111.

6. Thomas Merton, *Life and Holiness*, 4.

7. J. F. Hurst, *John Wesley the Methodist: A Plain Account of His Life and Work*, chap. 6: "To America and Back," (New York: The Methodist Book Concern, 1903), Wesley Center Online, http://wesley.nnu.edu/john-wesley/john -wesley-the-methodist/chapter-vi-to-america-and-back/.

8. *Journal of John Wesley*, http://www.ccel.org/ccel/wesley/journal.vi.ii.xvi .html.

9. "And Can It Be that I Should Gain," Charles Wesley, 1739, *The United Methodist Hymnal*, 363.

10. Everett Ferguson, *Baptism in the Early Church* (Grand Rapids: Eerdmans, 2009), 330.

11. Robert Farrar Capon, *The Parables of Grace* (Grand Rapids: Eerdmans, 1988), 44.

12. Steve Harper, "Lumen Fidei: Salvation by Faith," Oboedire, February 24, 2014, http://oboedire.wordpress.com/2014/02/24/lumen-fidei-salvation -by-faith/.

13. John Wesley, "Free Grace," http://www.umcmission.org/Find-Resources/ John-Wesley-Sermons/Sermon-128-Free-Grace#sthash.hskDa3hi.dpuf.

14. Ibid.

15. J. D. Walsh, "Wesley Vs. Whitefield," *Christianity Today*, April 1, 1993, http://www.ctlibrary.com/ch/1993/issue38/3834.html.

16. "Come, Sinners, to the Gospel Feast, Charles Wesley, 1747, *The United Methodist Hymnal*, 339.

17. E. Stanley Jones, *A Song of Ascents* (Nashville: Abingdon Press, 1968), 17.

Chapter 3

1. Eugene Peterson, *Practice Resurrection,* 198.

2. Magrey R. deVega, "Shall We Dance?" in *The Midweek Message,* St. Paul's United Methodist Church, Cherokee, Iowa, May 21, 2013, http://mdevega .blogspot.com/2013_05_01_archive.html.

3. "Perichoresis," http://www.merriam-webster.com/dictionary/perichoresis.

4. "Choreia," http://www.yourdictionary.com/chorea.

5. C. S. Lewis, *Mere Christianity* (New York: Macmillan, 1943; New York: Touchstone, 1996), 152.

6. Paul Young, *The Shack* (Newbury Park, CA: Windblown Media: 2007), 122.

7. Ibid., 124.

8. "Holy, Holy, Holy! Lord God Almighty," Reginald Heber, 1826, *The United Methodist Hymnal,* 64.

9. "Father, If Thou My Father Art," Charles Wesley, http://www.hymnary.org /text/father_if_thou_my_father_art.

10. Lewis, *Mere Christianity,* 176.

11. Augustine, *The Confessions,* trans. Maria Boulding (New York: Vintage Books, 1997), 6.

12. Heitzenrater, *Diary of an Oxford Methodist,* 168.

13. "Jesus, Thy Boundless Love to Me," Paul Gerhardt, 1653, trans. John Wesley, 1739, *The United Methodist Hymnal,* 183.

Chapter 4

1. Peterson, *Practice Resurrection,* 216.

2. Heitzenrater, *Diary of an Oxford Methodist,* 84.

3. Ibid.

4. http://www.state.gov/documents/organization/27807.pdf.

5. "The Pledge of Allegiance," http://www.ushistory.org/documents/pledge .htm.

6. Simon Critchley and Jamieson Webster, "The Gospel According to 'Me,'" *New York Times,* June 29, 2013, http://opinionator.blogs.nytimes. com/2013/06/29/the-gospel-according-to-me/?_php=true&_type =blogs&_r=0.

7. Jones, *A Song of Ascents*, 48.

8. Peter Storey, *And Are We Yet Alive* (Cape Town: Methodist Publishing House, 2004), 19.

9. Ibid, 41–42.

10. John Wesley, "The Catholic Spirit," http://wesley.nnu.edu/john-wesley /the-sermons-of-john-wesley-1872-edition/sermon-39-catholic-spirit/.

11. Chilcote, *John & Charles Wesley: Selections from Their Writings and Hymns*, 3.

12. "Phakamisa," http://www.phakamisa.org/.

Chapter 5

1. "Letter to Mr. George Shadford," *The Works of John Wesley*, ed. Thomas Jackson, XII: 457.

2. "O Thou Who Camest from Above," Charles Wesley, 1762, *The United Methodist Hymnal*, 501.

3. Frank Whaling, ed., *John and Charles Wesley: Selected Writings and Hymns* (Mahwah, NJ: Paulist Press, 1981), 81.

4. Sam Keen, *Fire in the Belly* (New York: Bantam, 1991), 61.

5. *Journal of John Wesley*, http://www.ccel.org/ccel/wesley/journal.vi.iii.i.html.

6. Storey, *And Are We Yet Alive*, 14.

7. John Wesley, "Upon Our Lord's Sermon on the Mount, 4, http://www .umcmission.org/Find-Resources/John-Wesley-Sermons/Sermon-24 -Upon-Our-Lords-Sermon-on-the-Mount-4#sthash.aXRfr81Z.dpuf.

8. Ibid.

9. Ibid.

10. Ibid.

11. Ibid.

12. Storey, *And Are We Yet Alive*, 29.

13. Shane Claiborne, "How Are We Political? A Dialogue Between Tony Campolo and Shane Claiborne," *Red Letter Christians*, October 30, 2012, http://www.redletterchristians.org/how-are-we-political-a-dialogue -between-tony-campolo-and-shane-claiborne/.

14. Fleming Rutledge, *And God Spoke to Abraham* (Grand Rapids: Eerdmans, 2011), 315.

15. Mark Binelli, "Pope Francis: The Times They Are A-Changin'," *Rolling Stone*, January 28, 2014, http://www.rollingstone.com/culture/news/pope -francis-the-times-they-are-a-changin-20140128#ixzz2ryjRRFAi.

Chapter 6

1. "Marching to Zion," Isaac Watts, 1707, *The United Methodist Hymnal*, 733.

2. *"Shir HaMa'alot,"* https://www.biblegateway.com/passage/?search =Tehillim+124%2CPsalm+124&version=OJB;NASB;MSG.

3. Jones, *A Song of Ascents*, 17.

4. Robert Browning, "Andrea del Sarto," http://www.poetryfoundation.org /poem/173001

5. Jones, *A Song of Ascents*, 18.

6. Heitzenrater, *Diary of an Oxford Methodist*, 45.

7. "A Word from Charles Wesley," #521 in *A Collection of Hymns for the Use of The People Called Methodists*, 1781, http://www.gbod.org/resources /a-word-from-charles-wesley.

8. "Love Divine, All Loves Excelling," Charles Wesley, 1747, *The United Methodist Hymnal*, 384.

9. Tom Johnson, "Take a Moment—Read Ted Kennedy's Eulogy of Bobby," ABC News *Nation*, August 26, 2009, http://abcnews.go.com/blogs /headlines/2009/08/take-a-moment-read-ted-kennedys-euology-of-bobby/.

10. "Thou, Jesu, Thou My Breast Inspire," Charles Wesley, http://www.invubu .com/lib/public/lyrics/show/Charles_Wesley/Thou%252C_Jesu%252C _Thou_My_Breast_Inspire.html.

11. "Love Divine, All Loves Excelling," Charles Wesley, 1747, *The United Methodist Hymnal*, 384.

NOTES

_____

_____

_____

_____

_____

_____

_____

_____

_____

_____

_____

_____

_____

_____

_____

_____

_____

_____

_____

_____

_____

NOTES

_____

_____

_____

_____

_____

_____

_____

_____

_____

_____

_____

_____

_____

_____

_____

_____

_____

_____

_____